D0394455

THE BOOK OF PERFECTLY PERILOUS MATH

THE BOOK OF PERFECTLY PERILOUS MATH

by Sean Connolly

WORKMAN PUBLISHING
NEW YORK

 Published simultaneously in Canada by Thomas Allen & Son Limited.

Library of Congress Cataloging-in-Publication Data is available.

ISBN 978-0-7611-6374-9

Design by Netta Rabin and Tae Won Yu
Cover and chapter opener illustrations by Allan Sanders
Method illustrations by Robb Allen
Math advisors: Kara Imm; George Hart, Museum of Mathematics

Workman Publishing Company, Inc.
225 Varick Street
New York, NY 10014-4381
www.workman.com

Printed in the United States of America

First printing March 2012
10 9 8 7 6 5 4 3 2 1

To Frederika, Jamie, Anna, Thomas, and Dafydd, who continue to help me sidestep perils—perfectly.

I am indebted to Raquel Jaramillo, Krestyna Lypen, and Netta Rabin of Workman Publishing as well as my agent, Jim Levine, for helping to solve the problems raised in—and by—this book. We can all take pride in the result. In addition, the following individuals and organizations provided inspiration, patient advice, or willing ears at every stage:

AAAS, Camco International, Gregory Etter, Dr. Gary Hoffman, Hostelling International, Professor Stewart Johnson, Dr. Peter Lydon, Massachusetts Institute of Technology, Professor Frank Morgan, Dr. Sarah Morse, Professor Jay Pasachoff, Ian Phipps, Peter Rielly, Elizabeth Stell, Nora Walsh, and Williams College Department of Mathematics and Statistics.

CONTENTS

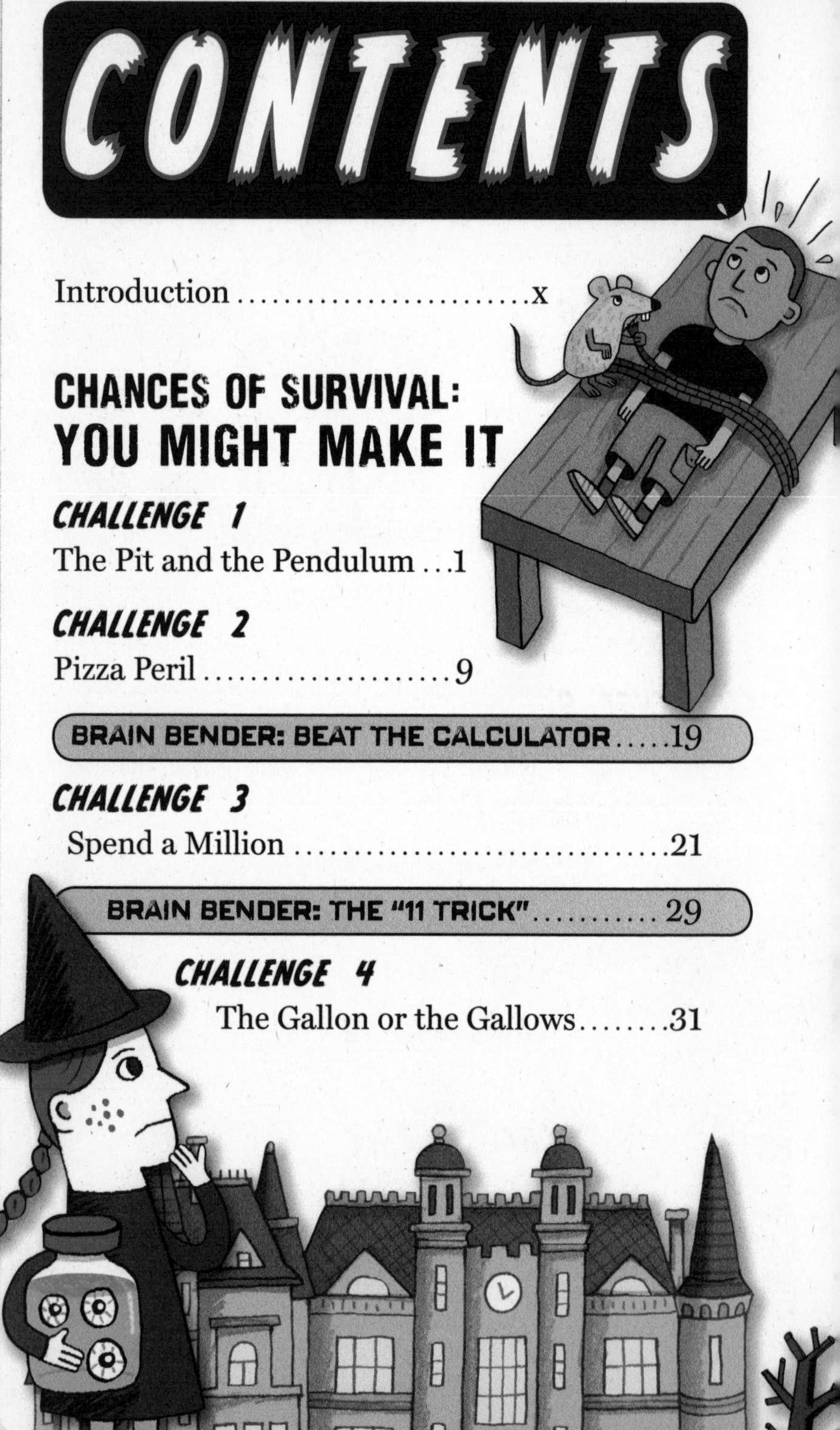

CHANCES OF SURVIVAL: SLIM TO NONE

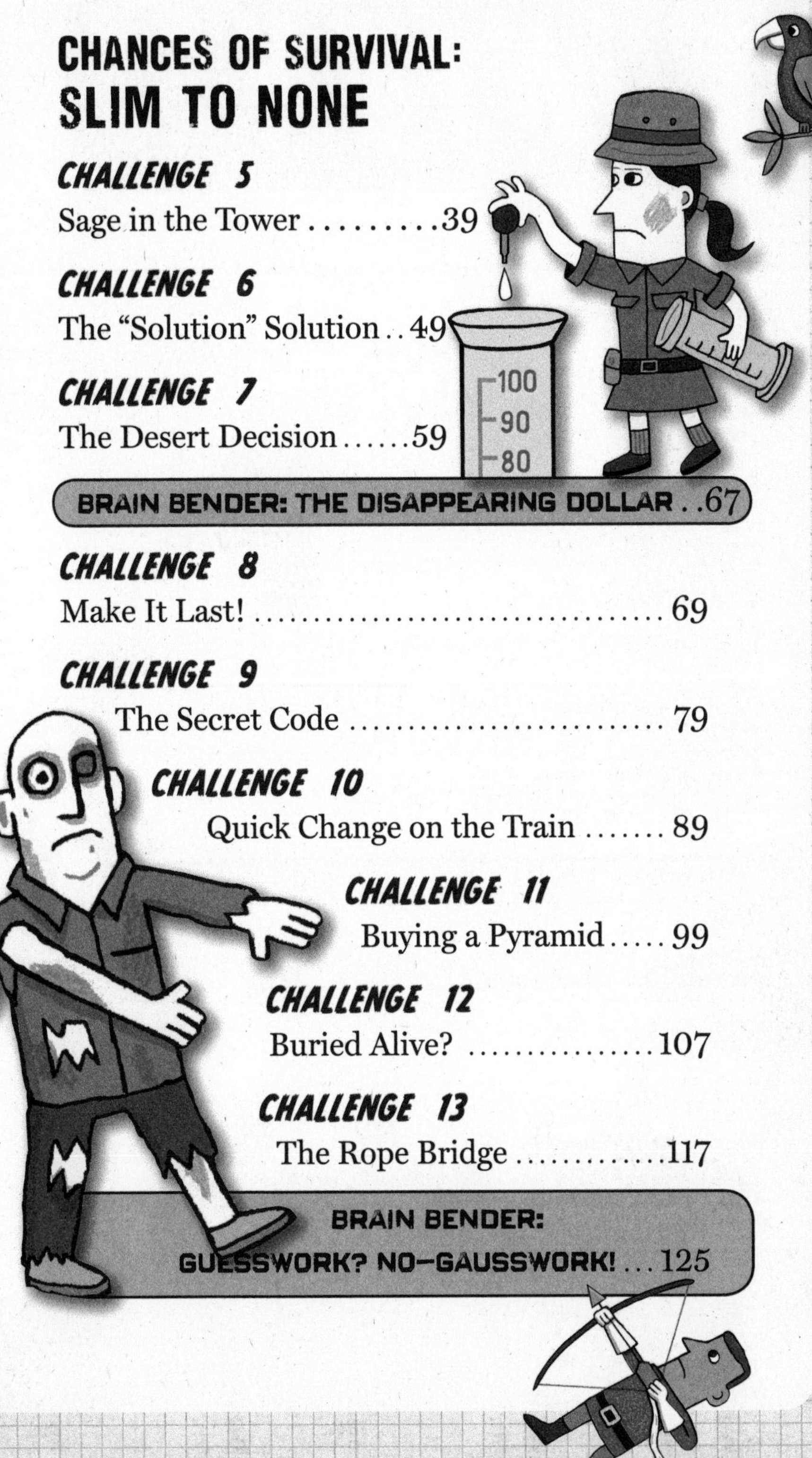

CHANCES OF SURVIVAL:
YOU'RE DEAD

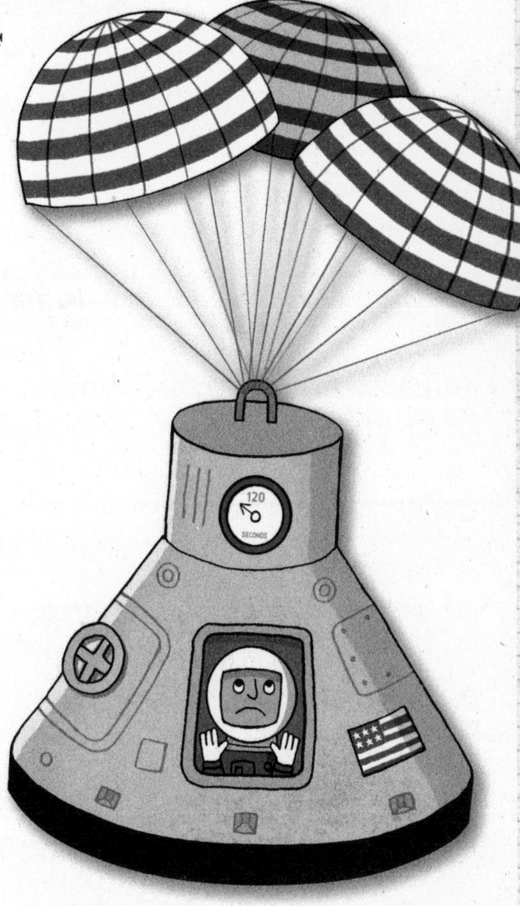
120
SECONDS

INTRODUCTION

The Book of Perfectly Perilous Math. Makes you think, doesn't it? "Perilous" has a dangerous ring to it. A perilous path probably snakes its way along a cliff top, with no guardrail and a river crashing its way through rapids hundreds of feet below you. Or maybe a perilous activity springs to mind, along the lines of sword-swallowing or free-fall skydiving.

Read through this book and you'll find perils of all descriptions—scuba tanks running low at a sunken shipwreck, international spy games on a lightning-fast train, blood-sucking vampires threatening to take over an entire town, painful bites from a deadly spider. Two things draw them all together, apart from the fact that they're all perilous. One is that a solution can be found using some basic math tools. And the other is that *you're* the one who has to find those tools and put them to use.

That's the "perilous" explained—but *perfectly*? What's that doing anywhere near the word "math"? It's not so strange, really. Think of a complicated division problem where you do all the work and you get the answer, with no remainder. Perfect! And you can take this perfect idea even further into math territory. The star pitcher who's clocked up all those zeroes—no runs, no hits, no bases on balls or errors—has just completed a perfect game. Those music standouts who can identify or exactly reproduce a particular note have "perfect pitch." Remember: Each musical note has its own frequency (numbers again!).

MATH IN REAL LIFE

The twenty-four challenges contained in *The Book of Perfectly Perilous Math* draw you into a world where all those math lessons meet real life. Sure, you've learned how much change to expect from a $5 bill if you buy two sodas and an ice-cream cone, but the challenges inside this book take you out of your comfort zone and into a world where life-threatening risks lie around every corner. You must summon your math skills just as you do whenever you pay for something or divide a pizza among friends . . . except this time the stakes are higher—much higher.

HOW THIS BOOK WORKS

Each of the challenges in *The Book of Perfectly Perilous Math* puts you in the hot seat. You're faced with a tough, maybe even do-or-die, problem that needs to be solved quickly. And that solution calls for all your math skills. Those same skills and concepts that you come across each day in math class take on a new meaning—they are now your survival skills.

- Probability? It just might help you decide which door to choose if your life depended on it: the one that will lead you to freedom, or the one that will lead you to an executioner's chambers.

- Powers of ten? Use them to make a lifesaving medicine to save a scientist in the jungle.

- The meaning of pi? It could make all the difference in creating a shield to save a planet from an asteroid hurtling through space.

Aligning with the Common Core Standards in mathematics for grades 5, 6, and 7, the problems are separated into three levels of difficulty, depending on your chances of survival: You Might Make It (grade 5), Slim to None (grade 6), and You're Dead (grade 7). The "Survival Strategies" for each problem clue you in on the math tools you'll need to use to make it through the danger.

Maybe you can jump in and find the right math tool to solve the problem. If not, then you can call on one of the greatest mathematicians of them all, Euclid. Each challenge includes a section called "Euclid's Advice," to help set you on the right track. You can think of Euclid as a helpful friend willing to whisper a hint in your ear.

Next comes "The Solution"—or at least our way of reaching the solution. Math problems can often be solved in different ways, and most require a series of steps, so think of this explanation as one road leading to the destination. Here is where you'll see all those math ideas working together just as they do in the classroom, but in new and exciting surroundings.

Each challenge finishes with a "Math Lab," a hands-on way of putting those math principles (the ones that led to the solution) into practice. The challenge that you just faced was perilous; with the Math Lab, it's time for some fun. Don't get the idea that you need all sorts of special equipment just because you see the word "lab." The Math Lab activities let you test and demonstrate those math principles using simple ingredients that you can find easily—such as sand, ice cream, a beach ball, construction paper, pinecones, and cornflakes.

And those "Brain Benders" scattered throughout? Those are just fun ways to see the cool things you can do with math! But that's enough explanation. It's time for you to tackle those perilous problems. Start reading . . . now!

01

CHANCES OF SURVIVAL: YOU MIGHT MAKE IT

SURVIVAL STRATEGIES: OPERATIONS AND ALGEBRAIC THINKING

DEATH BY: GIANT BLADE

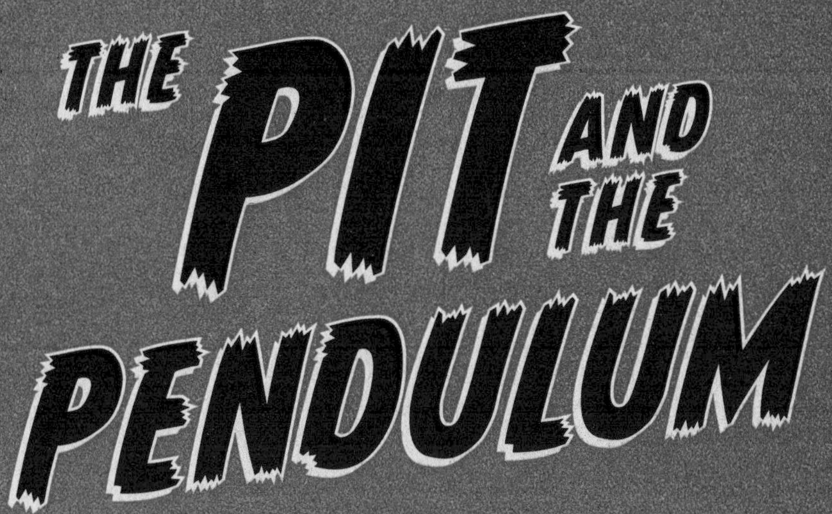

THE PIT AND THE PENDULUM

THE CHALLENGE

The year is 1714. You're in a dark Spanish prison. You wake up to find yourself tied to a table with ropes. In the darkness you hear a rhythmic swishing sound—something going back and forth, back and forth. Eventually your eyes get accustomed to the dark and see that the source of the sound is a sharp blade at the end of a long pendulum that's swinging back and forth over your body. With each sweep it gets a little lower—and a little closer to your chest.

You note how long it takes between those swishes: exactly 7 seconds. And with each swish, the blade drops 1 inch lower. The last passing was only 15 inches above your chest. It won't be much longer before the blade slices right through you.

Should you scream for help? That would probably just summon a guard, who would run you through with a sword then and there.

But wait! You see a rat by your arms and he's gnawing at the rope that binds you to the table. In fact, he has only 1 minute to go before he gnaws through it all the way. When he does that, you can get free!

Will the rat chew through the rope *before* or *after* the blade has slashed through your chest? How much time do you have exactly?

EUCLID'S ADVICE

You have all the information you need to solve the problem. Basically, it's a race between the rat and the blade on the pendulum.

- **You know how long it will take the rat to gnaw through the rope.**
- **You know how much more the blade must lower before it reaches you, how much it lowers with each swing, and how long it takes between swings.**

WORKSHEET

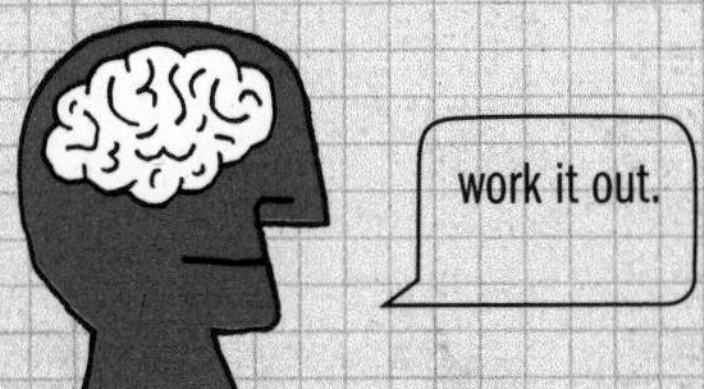

THE SOLUTION

THE RAT SHOULD CHEW THROUGH THE ROPE 45 SECONDS BEFORE THE PENDULUM BLADE REACHES YOUR CHEST.

Solve it, step-by-step:

1. You know that the rat will take 1 minute (60 seconds) to chew through the rope.

2. The pendulum blade is 15 inches above your chest and it lowers 1 inch with each swing. How many swings will it take the blade to reach you? Divide the height the blade is above you (15 inches) by the number of inches it drops per swing (1 inch).

$$15 \div 1 = 15 \text{ swings}$$

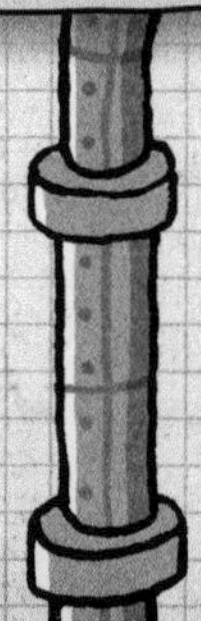

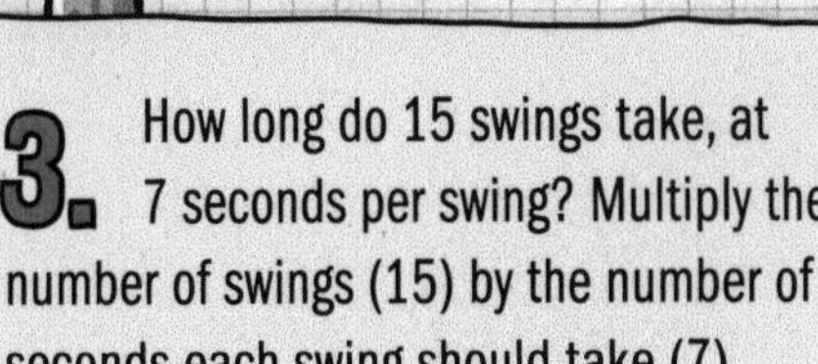

3. How long do 15 swings take, at 7 seconds per swing? Multiply the number of swings (15) by the number of seconds each swing should take (7).

$$15 \times 7 = 105 \text{ seconds}$$

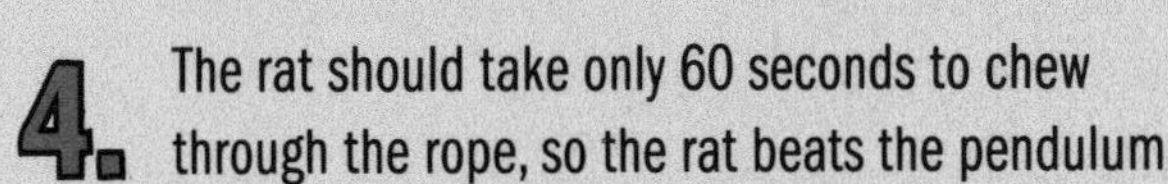

4. The rat should take only 60 seconds to chew through the rope, so the rat beats the pendulum!

5. To find out how much time you have to spare before the pendulum slashes through your chest, subtract the smaller amount of time (the rat's 60 seconds) from the larger amount of time (the pendulum's 105 seconds).

$$105 - 60 = 45 \text{ seconds}$$

You have 45 seconds to spare before the blade hits you.

Phew! Saved by the rat.

MATH LAB

Try this experiment to get an idea of how you can be so confident about pendulums and their movement.

YOU WILL NEED

- 36 INCHES OF STRING
- KEY
- SCISSORS
- 4 OR 5 HEAVY BOOKS
- TABLE AT LEAST 2½ FEET TALL
- RULER
- WATCH THAT CAN MEASURE SECONDS

THE METHOD

1. Take the 36-inch length of string and the key.

2. Loop one end of the string through the hole in the key and tie securely.

3. Cut off any excess string from the knot and center the knot on the top of the key, so that the key will hang straight, pointing down.

4. Pile the books on the table and slide the other end of the string under them.

5. Measure the section of string that is hanging down (your pendulum) and adjust it until it is 24 inches from the table edge to the bottom of the key. Slide the string under the books to raise or lower the pendulum.

6. Now pull the pendulum to the left about 12 inches, parallel to the table edge, and count how many times it passes the center in a minute.

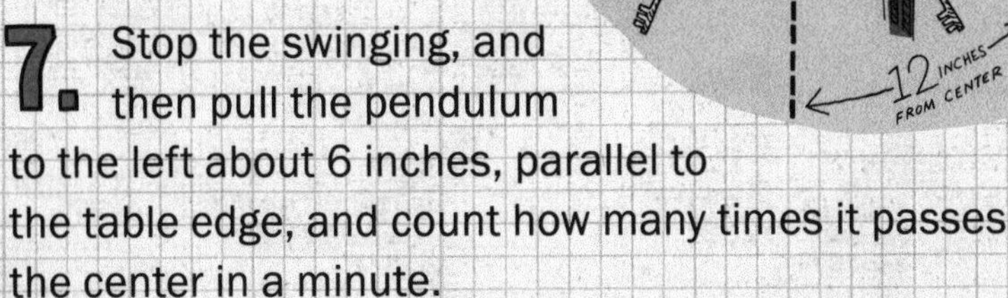

7. Stop the swinging, and then pull the pendulum to the left about 6 inches, parallel to the table edge, and count how many times it passes the center in a minute.

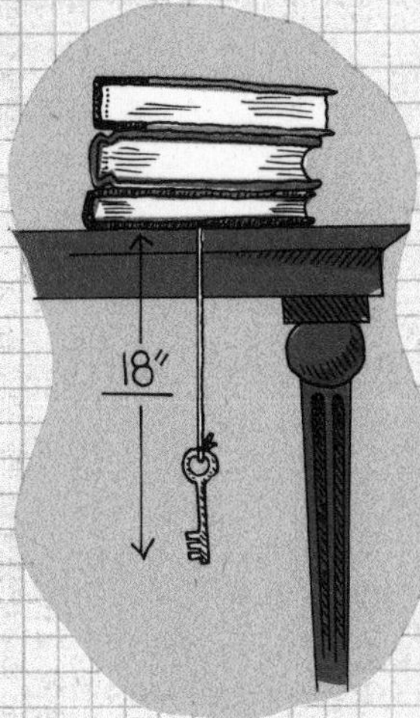

8. Now slide the string back through the books so that the pendulum hangs down 18 inches (instead of 24 inches).

9. Repeat steps 6 and 7.

10. What happens when you change the length of the string? What do your results tell you about the movement of pendulums in general?

THE SOLUTION: YOU SHOULD FIND THAT THE NUMBER OF TIMES A PENDULUM OF ANY PARTICULAR LENGTH (24 OR 18 INCHES, IN THIS EXPERIMENT) SWINGS BACK AND FORTH IN A GIVEN TIME (1 MINUTE, IN THIS EXPERIMENT) IS THE SAME, NO MATTER HOW FAR BACK AND FORTH IT SWINGS. THIS NUMBER IS AFFECTED ONLY BY THE LENGTH OF THE PENDULUM.

1/10
1/8
+
60
15
30
45
$90
×3
= 1/16
PEPPER
AVENU
Lunch
2
1/2
3

02

CHANCES OF SURVIVAL: YOU MIGHT MAKE IT

SURVIVAL STRATEGIES: FRACTIONS; EQUIVALENCE

DEATH BY: TERMINATION

THE CHALLENGE

It's your first day of work at *Catwalk* magazine, a dream come true. You're starting out as a lowly editorial assistant, but if you're patient and enthusiastic, then maybe one day you'll be flying off to Milan and Paris to check out the latest collections.

But that's still a daydream. For the moment you're the assistant to the glamorous

HOLD THE ANCHOVIES

We're used to choosing from dozens of toppings to go on our pizzas—whether they're thin-crust or deep-dish pizzas. Italians, though, often go for much simpler choices—maybe cheese and tomato or some sliced peppers on their pizzas.

Catwalk editor, Corey DiFerro—one of the toughest people in the business. People say that she chews up designers, photographers, receptionists—and probably editorial assistants—and spits them out. And you never did find out why the last editorial assistant at *Catwalk* lasted only one day.

You're outside the main editorial office when the door opens and someone calls to you, "Ms. DiFerro wants you—*now*!"

Inside, there's a group huddled around the main table. You recognize fashion designers, supermodels, two pop stars, photographers . . . and Corey DiFerro, looking you straight in the eye.

"Right. Do we have your attention? Look, we're off on a photo shoot in half an hour and we need some lunch first. Pizza—it's quick. Da Noi down on Seventh Avenue doesn't deliver, so I want you to go out and get some for us. Plain cheese only. Now, how hungry is everyone? I'll call your name and you tell my assistant how much you want."

"Scala twins?"

"One slice each."

"Art department?"

"Two pizzas."

"Gino?"

"Half a pizza."

"Copy editors?"

"We'll share one pizza."

"Arturo?"

"Three slices."

"Steve, our faithful driver?"

"One—one pizza, that is."

"And I'll have one slice," says Ms. DiFerro. She hands you a roll of bills and sends you off, saying, "They only take cash. Don't take too long."

On the elevator down, you count out the cash—$90 exactly. Will that be enough? You don't have any cash of your own in case you run short, and anyway, you don't have time to stop for more money.

At Da Noi you're standing on tiptoes to see over the other customers. Each pizza is cut into 12 slices—no exception. And the person ahead of you has just paid $36 for two pizzas.

It's your turn now. Will you have enough money—and will you have a job tomorrow?

EUCLID'S ADVICE

You need to find out two things: how much each pizza costs and how many slices make up a pizza.

- **The first part is easy enough: You know how much someone paid for two pizzas.**
- **The second part is simple—you know that Da Noi pizzas are cut into 12 equal slices.**
- **Now you have to put together all of the slices that were ordered to figure out how many more whole pizzas you need.**
- **Then add those "made up of slices" pizza(s) to the whole pizzas that others ordered to see how many you need overall.**

WORKSHEET

work it out.

THE SOLUTION

YOU'LL HAVE EXACTLY ENOUGH MONEY, BECAUSE YOU WILL NEED TO ORDER 5 PIZZAS, MAKING THE COST $90.

Solve it, step-by-step:

1. First, figure out how many pizzas you need to order. Remember, there are 12 slices per pie, so you can think of 1 slice of a pie (1 out of 12) as the fraction $\frac{1}{12}$.

List the whole pizzas first:

Art department	2 pizzas
Copy editors	1 pizza
Steve, the driver	1 pizza
Total:	**4 pizzas**

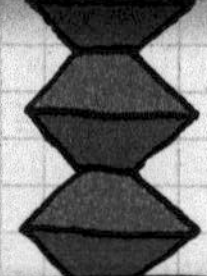

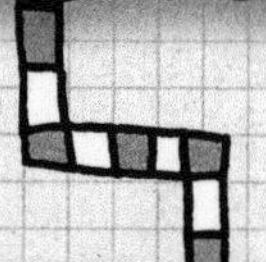

2. Now list the slices (in fractions):

Scala twins	2 slices ($\frac{2}{12}$)
Gino	6 slices ($\frac{6}{12}$)
Arturo	3 slices ($\frac{3}{12}$)
Corey DiFerro	1 slice ($\frac{1}{12}$)

3. Add up the slices:

$$\frac{2}{12} + \frac{6}{12} + \frac{3}{12} + \frac{1}{12} = \frac{12}{12} = 1$$

Total: 1 pizza

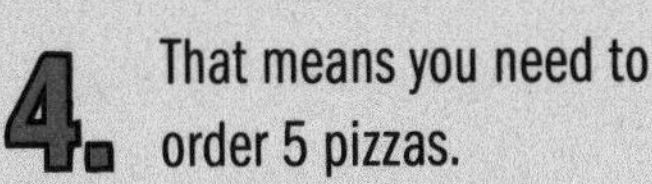

4. That means you need to order 5 pizzas.

$4 + 1 = 5$ pizzas

5. Next, figure out if you have enough money for 5 pizzas if 2 pizzas cost $36.

$36 \div 2 = \$18$ per pizza

$18 \times 5 = \$90$

That means 5 pizzas will cost you exactly $90. You have just enough money—for everyone else's lunch, that is.

MATH LAB

When you're ordering something like a pizza, it can get confusing trying to work out just how much you need. How big is a "large"? How small is a "small"? How many smalls would it take to make a large? What's better value—two small or one large pizza? Well, if you know the diameter of the pizzas, you can work it out yourself using a little math. Sometimes the result is surprising.

In this lab, you'll see that the area of two smaller circles (pretend they're small pizzas) is still less than the area of one large pizza—even though the width of each small pizza is more than half the width of the large pizza. You can work out the area of a circle by multiplying a special number called *pi* (which equals about 3.14) by the square of the radius of the circle. The symbol for pi (π) stands for the special constant that represents certain relationships within every circle.

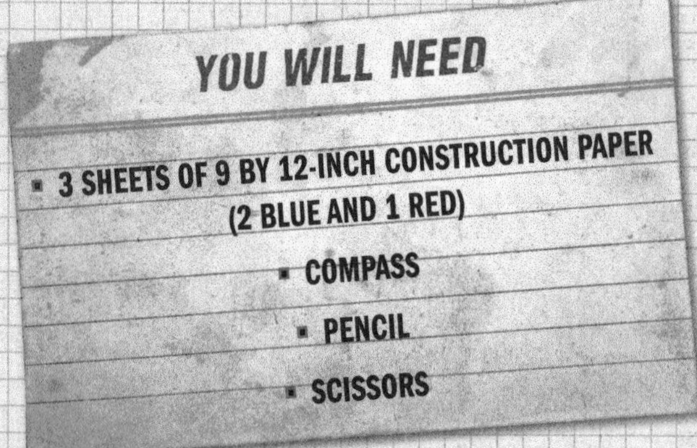

METHODS

1. Set a blue piece of paper on a table or desk and use the compass to trace a circle that has a radius of 2 inches.

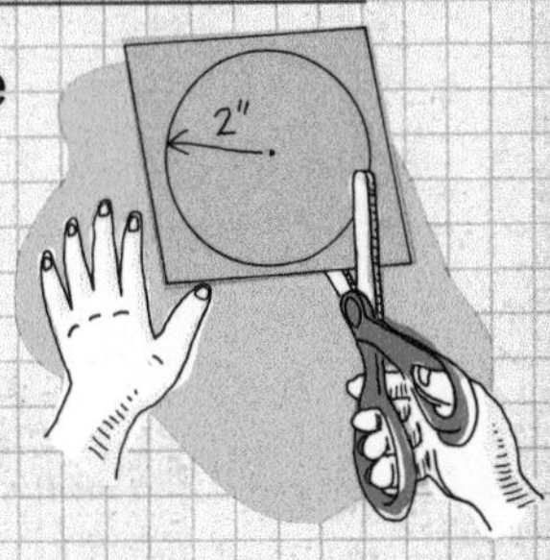

2. Cut out that circle and set it aside.

3. With the second piece of blue paper, repeat steps 1 and 2.

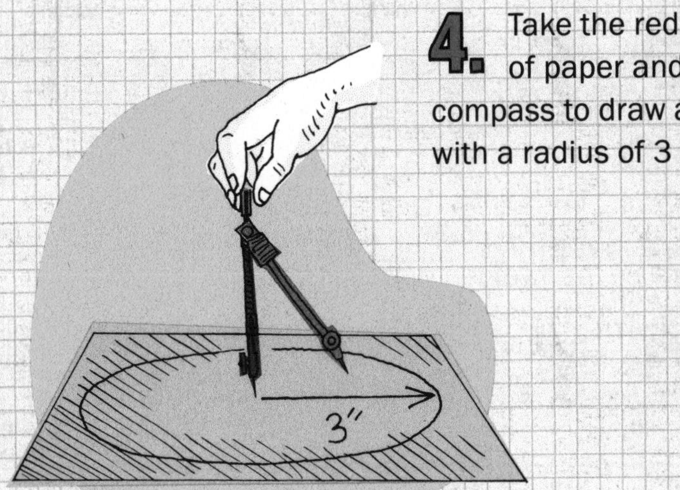

4. Take the red piece of paper and use the compass to draw a circle with a radius of 3 inches.

5. Cut that circle out.

6. Now try to put both blue circles inside the larger, red circle without having any portions of the blue circles overlapping. Do this by cutting off pieces of the blue circles and placing them wherever there's still red showing.

7. When you've fully taken apart the blue circles and placed them in the red circle without any overlapping, you should still have some red showing. This proves that the area of the larger circle is still larger than the combined areas of the smaller circles.

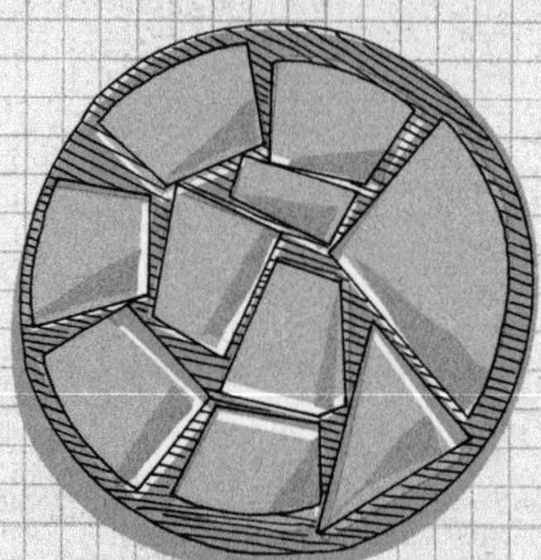

8. Of course, you could have saved yourself a lot of measuring and cutting by using math to show how the areas of the circles matched up. Use the following equation to determine the area of a circle:

$$\text{Area} = \text{pi} \times \text{radius squared}$$
$$(\text{or, } A = \pi r^2)$$

and you'll see that the area of the large (red) circle (which had a radius of 3 inches) is

$$\pi \times 3^2$$
$$3.14 \times 9 = 28.26 \text{ square inches}$$

The area of each smaller (blue) circle is

$$\pi \times 2^2$$
$$3.14 \times 4 = 12.56 \text{ square inches}$$

Twice that figure makes 25.12 square inches, which is still smaller than the area of the larger (red) circle.

BRAIN BENDER

BEAT THE CALCULATOR

Here's a quick trick you can play on a friend. Make sure she has a calculator and tell her that you're going to have a race—she with the calculator against you doing mental arithmetic. All you have is a pencil and paper to write down your answer. Now find a calendar and open it to any month.

Ask your friend to draw (or imagine) a 3-by-3-inch square around any nine dates on the calendar. Let's say she has selected:

12	13	14
19	20	21
26	27	28

Make sure she has her calculator turned on and ask her to add up those nine numbers. Meanwhile you can write down "180" on the slip of paper and turn it facedown. In about a minute, she'll show you her answer (also "180"). You can then reveal your own.

Try it again with another nine dates and you'll still beat her. And again. And again. Why? Because you've simply multiplied the middle date ("20" in the example) by 9. And if you want a hint about multiplying by 9, just remember to multiply by 10 (just add a digit zero—"0") and then subtract the number. So 20 × 9 is the same as 20 × 10 (200) minus 20 . . . or 180!

42
003
022
X450
Y789
ZONE
B

03

CHANCES OF SURVIVAL: YOU MIGHT MAKE IT

SURVIVAL STRATEGIES: NUMBERS AND OPERATIONS IN BASE 10

DEATH BY: LASERS

SPEND A MILLION

THE CHALLENGE

"You have entered Zone B, which is forbidden to all but official badge holders. Negative badge-recognition. Isolation exercise now in effect."

What's going on?! You were racing your pal Jasmine on your mountain bikes and you thought you'd found a clever shortcut through this industrial park on the edge of the canyon. All of a sudden, a hologram of a robot is in front of you and you're trapped by laser beams.

"Very funny, Jasmine," you yell. "Call off the laser pointers."

"Negative badge-recognition. Isolation exercise now in effect. Password, please."

"I'm Andy Turner. I'm sorry, I don't know anything about recognition or passwords."

" 'I'm Andy Turner' not recognized. Exit permission consideration mode. Andy Turner—do you agree to undertake a question to secure release?"

"Yes. Anything!"

"Affirmative. Here is the challenge: You have 1 million dollars. You spend 50 cents every second. How many days will it take you to run out of money? Round up or down to the nearest whole number. You have 2 minutes to answer, which commences now!"

And with the word "now," an empty soda can gets zapped—and disappears. It's pressure time.

How long will it take you to spend $1,000,000 if you spend it at a rate of 50¢ every second, making sure to round to the nearest whole number?

EUCLID'S ADVICE

You're working your way up through units of time here, from seconds to days, so that's the route that your solution should take.

Write down everything you know:

- **The rate per second is 50¢.**
- **From that you can work out the amount you'd spend in a minute, and then the amount per hour, and then the amount per day.**
- **Remember to round up or down to the nearest whole number.**

WORKSHEET

THE SOLUTION

IT WILL TAKE YOU 23 DAYS TO SPEND 1 MILLION DOLLARS AT THAT RATE.

Solve it, step-by-step:

1. You know that the rate is 50¢ per second. First, find out how much you'd spend in 1 minute. Multiply \$0.50 by 60 seconds.

$$\$0.50 \times 60 = \$30$$

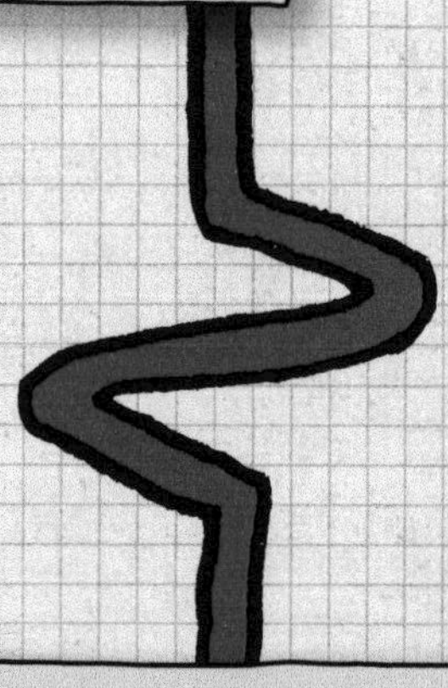

2. Next, find out how much you'd spend in 1 hour. Multiply \$30 by 60 minutes.

$$\$30 \times 60 = \$1,800$$

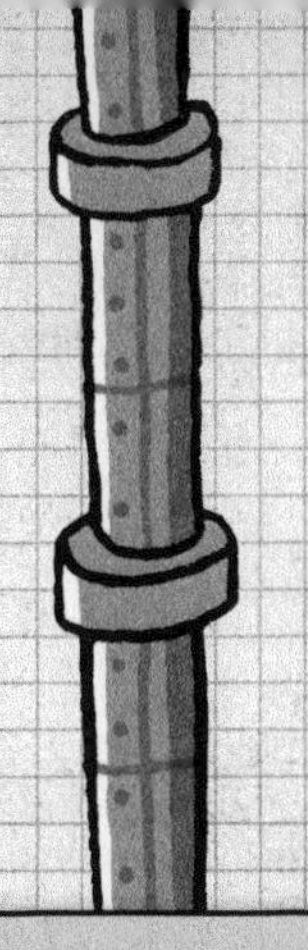

3. Then find out how much you'd spend in 1 day. Multiply \$1,800 by 24 hours.

$$\$1,800 \times 24 = \$43,200$$

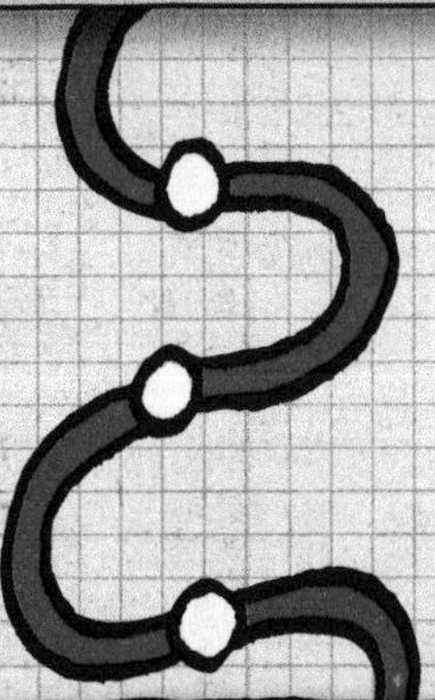

4. Now that you know you'd spend \$43,200 in 1 day, you can figure out how many days it will take you to spend all 1 million dollars. Divide \$1,000,000 by \$43,200.

$$\$1,000,000 \div \$43,200 = 23.\overline{148}$$

That means it will take you a little more than 23 days to spend all of the money. But since the robot asked you to round up or down to the nearest whole number, the answer is 23 days!

MATH LAB

Here's a way that you and your friends can simulate spending 1 million dollars—or even 1 billion dollars—in your own kitchen . . . using jelly beans. In fact, you could use cornflakes, marbles, or anything else you choose to represent money. The main thing is to work out how many dollars each of the objects represents and how fast you can transfer them from one side of the room to the other.

This game works best in a large room—or even outside.

YOU WILL NEED

- 1 LARGE MIXING BOWL
- JELLY BEANS (ENOUGH TO FILL HALF THE MIXING BOWL), OR MARBLES, CORNFLAKES, ETC.
- 3 PLASTIC CUPS
- FRIENDS (AT LEAST ONE OTHER PERSON)
- WATCH OR TIMER

THE METHOD

1. Fill the mixing bowl halfway up with jelly beans.

2. Put the bowl on the floor on one side of the room.

3. Put the 3 empty cups side by side on the floor on the other side of the room (at least 15 paces away from the bowl).

4. Get someone to act as the timer: They need to do three 1-minute timings.

5. Have the first person stand by the empty cups, and on a signal, she or he should go to the bowl, pick up 1 jelly bean, and place it in one of the cups, working at a steady pace.

6. The person continues to collect and deposit jelly beans in that cup until the timer calls out 1 minute.

7. The player then repeats steps 5 and 6, filling up a second cup . . . and then a third cup.

8. Find the average number of jelly beans collected in a cup. This gives the average number of jelly beans collected per minute.

9. Repeat steps 5 through 8 for each player.

10. Now imagine that each jelly bean is worth $10. If each player could collect $10 jelly beans for as long as she liked, how long would it take each player to make one million dollars?

11. Can you work out how long it would take to become a billionaire?

THE SOLUTION: TO FIND THE AVERAGE NUMBER OF JELLY BEANS IN A CUP: COUNT THE BEANS IN EACH CUP, ADD THOSE NUMBERS TOGETHER, AND DIVIDE BY 3. THIS WILL GIVE YOU THE AVERAGE NUMBER OF BEANS COLLECTED PER MINUTE (AND PER CUP). TO FIND OUT HOW LONG IT WOULD TAKE EACH PLAYER TO SPEND 1 MILLION DOLLARS, OR 1 BILLION DOLLARS, FOLLOW THE SOLUTION TECHNIQUES IN THE "SPEND A MILLION" CHALLENGE ON PAGES 24–25.

BRAIN BENDER

THE "11 TRICK"

Everyone knows there's a simple rule about multiplying a number by 10—add a digit zero! So 34 × 10 becomes 340 and 46 × 10 is 460. But did you know that you can work out how to multiply any 2-digit number, such as 34, by 11?

Here's what you do. Instead of adding something (like a zero) to the end of that 2-digit number, you add something to the *middle* of it. First you imagine that you pull the digits of that original number apart, leaving a gap inside, so 34 becomes 3__4.

Then you add the digits of that 2-digit number together and slot the result into the gap you left earlier, so 3 + 4 = 7. Put that "7" into the gap and you get 374. Which is exactly what 34 × 11 equals!

One thing to remember, though, is that if the sum of the two digits comes to more than 9, then you write the "ones" digit in the gap and "carry" the "tens" digit.

Try it with 46 × 11. First pull them apart, to get 4__6. Then do the addition: 4 + 6 = 10.

Then plug the "ones" digit ("0") into the gap, and carry over the tens digit ("1") . The result is 506, which we know is the same as 46 × 11!

If you look at how to multiply 46 × 11, you can see why this trick works:

$$\begin{array}{r} 46 \\ \times 11 \\ \hline 46 \\ +46 \\ \hline 506 \end{array}$$

3 Qt
5 Qt

04

CHANCES OF SURVIVAL: YOU MIGHT MAKE IT

SURVIVAL STRATEGIES: QUANTITATIVE AND ABSTRACT REASONING

DEATH BY: VEXED PARENTS

THE GALLON OR THE GALLOWS

THE CHALLENGE

"Let's see. We need 3 toad eyes, 27 hairs from an elephant, 1 ounce of dragon blood, a pinch of paprika, 1 tiger tooth, 13 four-leaf clovers, and *exactly* 1 gallon of water. Hurry, please, or you will regret it!"

The head witch's words ring in your ears as she sends you from the school to gather the ingredients for the invisibility potion.

You can't mess this up! The head witch has already threatened to expel you after your levitating spell went awry—it took forever to get all of the classroom's furniture off of the ceiling.

You walk to the mystical shops in the village a few miles away to purchase all of the ingredients, and then stop at the well. Oh no! You forgot the gallon container in your rush out the door! And you need to deliver exactly 1 gallon of water or the potion won't work. You can't get expelled. Your parents will freak out! There must be a way . . . wait! Two buckets are hanging by the well. One of them holds exactly 3 quarts and the other holds exactly 5 quarts. Other than "3 quart" and "5 quart" labels, they bear no other markings.

Since a gallon is 4 quarts, can you work out a series of steps that will allow you to make use of these buckets to collect 1 gallon?

EUCLID'S ADVICE

This problem calls for a bit of logic. You need to return with exactly 1 gallon (4 quarts) of water.

- **You could try to find a way of carrying back the smaller (3-quart) bucket $\frac{2}{3}$ full and the larger (5-quart) bucket $\frac{2}{5}$ full but the buckets have no markings, so you have no way of accurately measuring the portions of water.**
- **The same would be true of any combination of partly filled buckets—or trying to estimate $\frac{4}{5}$ of the bigger bucket (4 quarts).**
- **The answer will have to involve filling the larger bucket with 4 quarts of water.**
- **You can measure out 3 quarts accurately, so the question is now how to measure out an additional 1 quart.**
- **Sometimes a solution involves working backward: Think of some way that dumping water out could lead to the answer.**

WORKSHEET

THE SOLUTION

THE LARGER BUCKET CAN BE FILLED IN 2 STAGES: FIRST, WITH 1 QUART OF WATER, AND THEN WITH 3 QUARTS OF WATER.

Solve it, step-by-step:

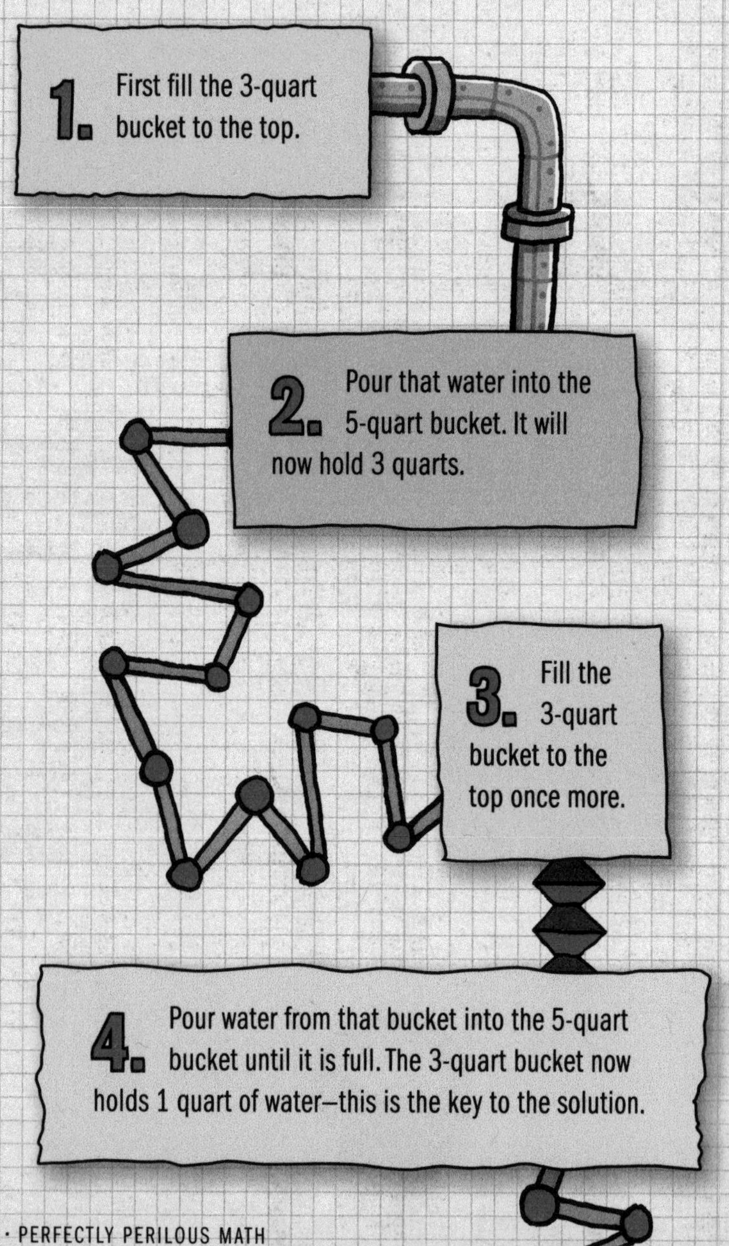

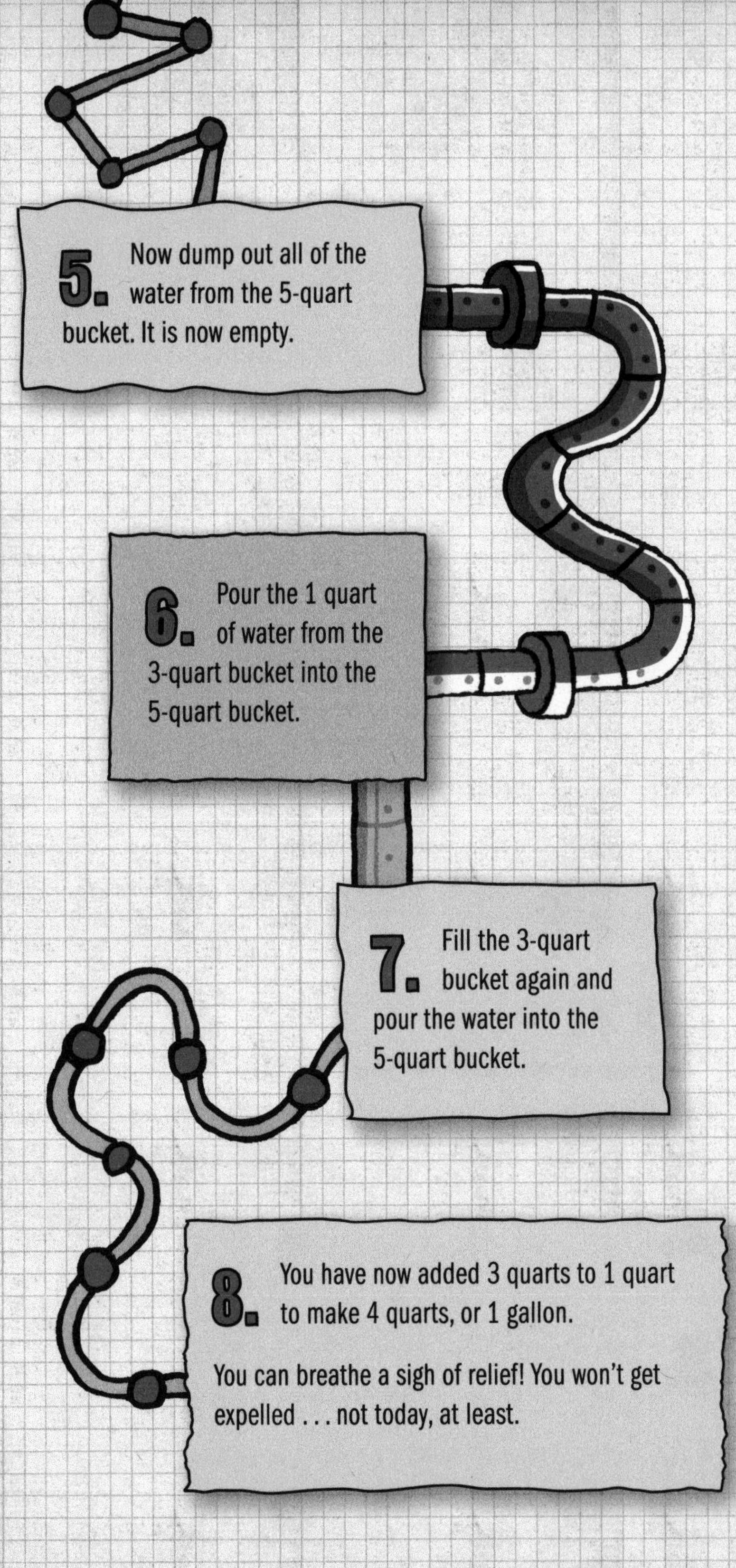
5. Now dump out all of the water from the 5-quart bucket. It is now empty.
6. Pour the 1 quart of water from the 3-quart bucket into the 5-quart bucket.
7. Fill the 3-quart bucket again and pour the water into the 5-quart bucket.
8. You have now added 3 quarts to 1 quart to make 4 quarts, or 1 gallon.
You can breathe a sigh of relief! You won't get expelled . . . not today, at least.

MATH LAB

The gallon challenge is a great way to become even more confident with measurements. Because, as you'll see, even if a measuring cup is "full," there may still be room for more. How could this be?

It's all about what you're measuring, as you'll see with this simple activity.

YOU WILL NEED

- TWO 1-CUP MEASURING CUPS
- WATER
- 1 PINT (GIVE OR TAKE) OF SAND OR GRAVEL
- 40 TO 50 MARBLES
- LARGE SPOON

THE METHOD

1. Fill one measuring cup with water to the 1-cup level exactly.
2. Fill the other measuring cup with sand or gravel to the 1-cup level exactly.
3. You should now have 1 level cup of water and 1 level cup of either sand or gravel.

4. Now pour a little of the water into the cup of sand or gravel.

5. Keep pouring water into the other cup slowly until the water can be seen at the 1-cup level.

6. Check on the level of water remaining in the "water" cup. Why do you think that you could pour so much water into the other cup?

7. Now empty and rinse out the cups and do the same experiment, replacing sand or gravel with marbles. Can you pour as much water into the cup now? Why or why not?

8. Empty the cups and do the experiment in reverse, spooning sand or gravel (or marbles) into the cup full of water. What happened? Can you explain the difference in the experiments?

THE SOLUTION: IT ALL COMES DOWN TO MATTER. A LIQUID, LIKE WATER, WILL TAKE UP ALL OF THE SPACE IN THE MEASURING CUP. SOLIDS LIKE SAND OR MARBLES WILL HAVE GAPS IN BETWEEN INDIVIDUAL PIECES WHEN GROUPED TOGETHER. WHEN YOU ADD WATER TO A MEASURING CUP FILLED WITH SAND OR MARBLES, YOU ARE FILLING IN THOSE GAPS, ALLOWING YOU TO FIT "MORE THAN" 1 CUP!

05

CHANCES OF SURVIVAL: SLIM TO NONE

SURVIVAL STRATEGIES: RATIOS AND PROPORTIONS; GEOMETRY

DEATH BY: ENEMY KNIGHTS

SAGE IN THE TOWER

THE CHALLENGE

You are on your way to rescue your king's most trusted scholar, who is said to be able to make mathematical calculations at lightning speeds in her head without needing to write down the numbers. Someone that brilliant is of great use to kings and emperors, of course, so it's not strange that the sage should have been captured by the enemy king.

BRIDGE OF SMOOTS

A group of students at the Massachusetts Institute of Technology (MIT) invented a new measurement on a winter night in 1958. They used a freshman, Oliver Smoot, to measure the length of a bridge across the Charles River in Boston. Literally! They carried him across the bridge, marking out how many of his body lengths they traveled. They called this new measurement a "smoot"—partly in honor of the willing freshman and partly because they felt that the name "sounded scientific, like watt or amp."

MIT students continue to paint in the 10-smoot markers right to the end of the bridge, which is marked "364.4 smoots and one ear."

You realize you're being chased by enemy knights as you approach the tower where the king's scholar is being kept. It's a bright sunny day, the ground ahead of you is flat and easy to travel, and you have a perfect view of the top of the tower.

But, there's no ladder in sight! As the knights close in, you begin to feel defeated . . . until, wait! You'll knot together a rope made out of those extra sheets you packed in your bag, and use your trusty longbow to send one end of the rope to the top of the tower so the scholar can climb down. But how long does the rope need to be? There's no time for trial and error.

What do you know? You're exactly the same height as your 5-foot longbow, and your shadow is exactly the same length as 2.5 longbows. You get an idea and measure the length of the tower's shadow: 20 longbows. Yes, you've got enough information to figure out how tall the tower is now!

How tall is the tower? How long should you make the rope of sheets to rescue the king's scholar?

SHADOWS AND PROPORTIONS

A sunny day, any flat surface, and an object casting a shadow are the main ingredients for using triangles to solve "real world" proportions. The height of the object is one side, the shadow it casts is another, and the angle at which a ray of sun hits the ground is the third. Taking for granted that the ground is flat, this triangle is a right-angled triangle. And remember that the sun's rays travel parallel lines to the ground. That means that if you have the height of one object, and can measure its shadow, you can find the height of a second object with a measurable shadow nearby. Why? Because of the conditions, you'll have similar triangles, which means the sides are in proportion to one another. Just set up proportional fractions and solve for the missing side.

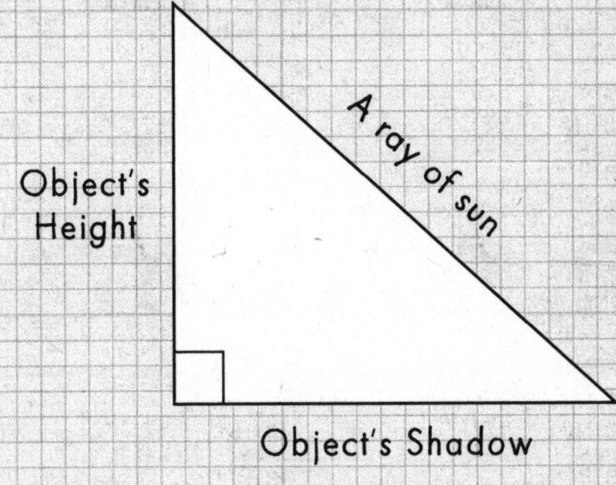

EUCLID'S ADVICE

Write down everything you know:

- **It's a sunny day, so you can see your shadow. That means everything around you is casting a shadow.**
- **You used your 5-foot longbow to measure your height (1 longbow), your shadow (2.5 longbows), and the tower's shadow (20 longbows).**
- **With this information, you can draw two similar triangles, and create a proportion problem to solve for the missing side.**

WORKSHEET

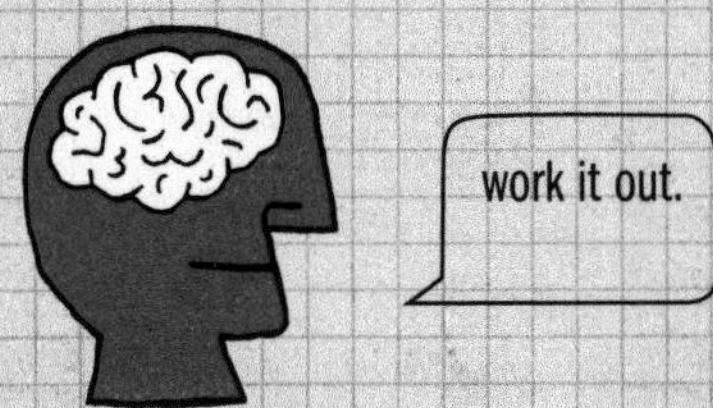
work it out.

THE SOLUTION

THE TOWER IS 40 FEET (8 LONGBOWS) TALL, SO YOUR ROPE SHOULD BE 40 FEET LONG.

Solve it, step-by-step:

1. With the given information, you can set up a proportion problem using two similar triangles to solve for the height of the tower.

Triangle 1 consists of you (1 longbow tall = 1 × 5 = 5 feet tall), your shadow (2.5 longbows long = 2.5 × 5 = 12.5 feet long), and a ray of sun (you don't need to know the length of this side since it is parallel to the equivalent side on the second triangle).

Triangle 2 consists of the tower (let's call this variable *h*), the tower's shadow (20 × 5 = 100 feet long), and a ray of sun (again, you don't need to know this length).

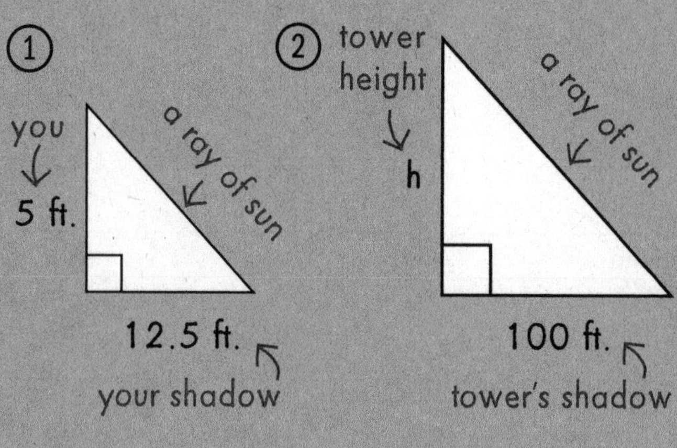

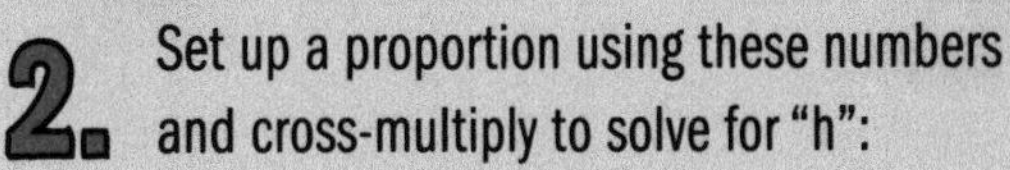

2. Set up a proportion using these numbers and cross-multiply to solve for "h":

$$\frac{5}{12.5} = \frac{h}{100}$$

$$500 = 12.5h$$

$$h = 40 \text{ feet}$$

That means that the height of the tower is 40 feet tall (or 40 ÷ 5 = 8 longbows). Your quick thinking saved the sage!

You can also use the concept of similar triangles to measure the height of a tall tree, lamppost, or flagpole. Try this activity in a flat section of a park, on a sidewalk, or in a schoolyard on a sunny day when you're sure to have shadows. If you do it in late morning or early afternoon, when the shadows are shortest, some of the calculations will be easier.

YOU WILL NEED

- TREE (OR LAMPPOST OR FLAGPOLE) WITH OPEN SPACE NEAR IT
- FRIEND TO HELP YOU MEASURE
- TAPE MEASURE (OR YARDSTICK)

THE METHOD

1. Find a tree (or lamppost or flagpole) whose shadow falls completely on level ground (make sure there aren't any benches, grills, or picnickers in the way).

2. Stand next to the tree and ask your friend to measure the length of your shadow, and then your height (use inches for both measurements). These represent two sides (the height and length) of the first triangle.

3. Now measure the length of the tree's shadow—in feet. This represents one side (the length) of the second triangle. Assign a variable for the height of the tree (let's call it h).

4. Set up a proportion using these numbers and cross-multiply to solve for h to find out how tall the object is in feet.

$$\frac{\text{your height}}{\text{your shadow's length}} = \frac{h}{\text{the object's shadow length}}$$

100
90
80
70
60
50
40
30
20
10
DO NOT OPEN

06

CHANCES OF SURVIVAL: SLIM TO NONE

SURVIVAL STRATEGIES: RATIOS AND PROPORTIONS

DEATH BY: SPIDER BITE

THE "SOLUTION" SOLUTION

THE CHALLENGE

You're assisting Dr. Grog, a world-famous scientist, on a mission to identify new species of insects and spiders in the mountains of Costa Rica. You and Dr. Grog have been "in the bush" for four days, gathering notes and taking photographs, capturing insects, and identifying habitats.

MIXING CYLINDERS

A mixing cylinder, sometimes called a graduated cylinder, is a piece of scientific equipment used to make accurate measurements of liquids. It is made of a durable, clear material like high-tech plastic or shatterproof glass and is marked along the side for accurate readings of measurements. Most mixing cylinders are marked in liters, centiliters, and milliliters because scientists use metric measurements rather than American measurements such as pints and fluid ounces.

Your job is to collect water from the inside of flower blossoms. These water samples will be studied later under the microscope to identify the tiny creatures that insects feed on. It's a delicate operation that involves sucking up water with small eye droppers, filling 10-milliliter (10 ml) sample spoons until they are full (10 drops), and pouring each spoonful into 100-ml mixing cylinders.

Just when things seemed to be getting a little boring, you're hit with a critical emergency. Dr. Grog has been bitten by a Brazilian wandering spider, the deadliest in the world. People can die from one of its bites unless they are given antivenin immediately—the problem is that the only person who has been trained to administer the serum is now unconscious!

It's time to act fast. You find the antivenin serum in the first-aid kit. The directions say that you have to put 3 drops of serum on Dr. Grog's tongue within 7 minutes, but in a concentration of 1 part per million. If it's stronger than that, it will kill him. If it's weaker than that, he'll die from the spider's venom.

Can you figure out a series of steps that will allow you to dilute the full-strength serum to 1 part per million?

RATIOS

A ratio is simply a comparison of two things in relation to one another. So, if you have two ladybugs and five flowers, the ratio of ladybugs to flowers is 2 to 5 (or 2:5, or $\frac{2}{5}$). What about in terms of a solution, like the antidote in the problem? It's just the same! If you put 1 ml of juice in a 100 ml container of water, the ratio of juice to water is 1 to 100 (or 1 part per 100, or 1:100, or $\frac{1}{100}$).

EUCLID'S ADVICE

The metric system, even if it seems unfamiliar, will help you here because it works in tens, hundreds, and thousands—not in twos, fours, twelves, and sixteens like the U.S. system.

Write down everything you know:

- **You're starting out with a serum that's a million times too strong. In other words, it has to be diluted so that it becomes a million times weaker. Luckily, you have some tools to help you do this: eye droppers, 10-ml sample spoons, and a 100-ml mixing cylinder. How can they help?**
- **You know how many drops of liquid fill the 10-ml spoon: 10. That means 1 drop equals 1 ml.**
- **The mixing cylinder holds 100 ml, so if you squeezed 1 drop of serum into a cylinder full of water, you would have weakened it 100 times. In other words, it would now be 1 part per 100.**

How can you use this information to move ahead?

WORKSHEET

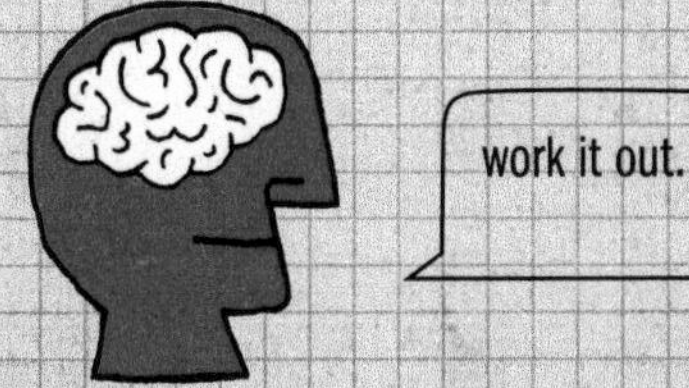
work it out.

THE SOLUTION

YOU CAN ARRIVE AT A LIQUID THAT'S 1 MILLION TIMES WEAKER BY A SERIES OF STAGES USING EYE DROPPERS, SERUM, A MIXING CYLINDER, AND WATER.

Solve it, step-by-step:

1. Fill the mixing cylinder with 100 ml of water.

2. Use an eye dropper to squeeze out 1 drop of the antivenin into the cylinder. Since you know that 1 drop equals 1 ml of solution, you now have a solution that is 1 part per 100, or 1 : 100. Empty the rest of the serum from the eye dropper back into the original bottle.

3. Use a clean eye dropper to collect some of the new 1 : 100 solution; then pour out the rest of the solution left inside the mixing cylinder. Rinse and refill the cylinder with 100 ml of water.

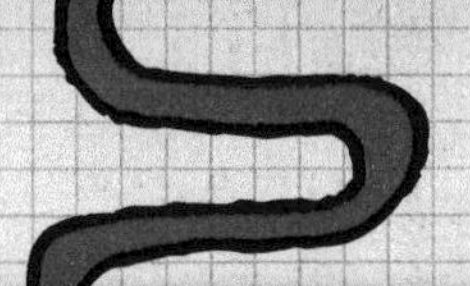

4. Use your eye dropper to squeeze out 1 drop of the 1 : 100 solution into the cylinder. Now the cylinder is a solution that is 1 part per 10,000, or 1 : 10,000. Why? To get the new strength of the solution, multiply the strength of the solution in the eye dropper ($\frac{1}{100}$) by the new strength of the solution in the mixing cylinder ($\frac{1}{100}$).

$$\frac{1}{100} \times \frac{1}{100} = \frac{1}{10{,}000}$$

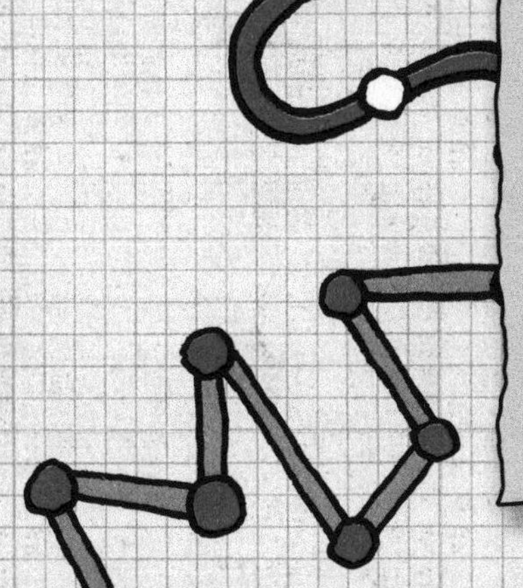

5. Use another eye dropper to collect some of the 1 : 10,000 solution; then pour out the rest of the solution left inside the mixing cylinder. Rinse and refill the cylinder with 100 ml of water.

6. Use your eye dropper to squeeze 1 drop of the 1 : 10,000 solution into the cylinder. Now the solution is . . . what?

$$\frac{1}{100} \times \frac{1}{10{,}000} = \frac{1}{1{,}000{,}000}$$

The solution is 1 part per 1,000,000.

Yay, you've saved Dr. Grog!

The problem you just solved (and this experiment!) calls on some simple math to save time and effort to reach the target concentration of 1 part per million. You could have put a teaspoon of juice in a barrel and then added a million spoonfuls of water to reach the same concentration. While this is a fine strategy, it takes time, lots of water, and a very large container. Instead, you can do it in stages.

A liquid that mixes with another liquid (like juice into water) is said to be *in solution*. Scientists use numbers to describe the strength of a solution. A shark can detect blood in a solution of 1 part per million (1 ppm)—that's 1 drop of blood mixed with 1 million drops of water. You can demonstrate what a 1-ppm solution is like with the following simple experiment. (Note that since a pint is actually 96 teaspoons, not 100, this experiment is an approximation of 1-ppm.)

YOU WILL NEED

- RED JUICE, LIKE TOMATO OR CRANBERRY
- CUP OR GLASS
- THREE 1-PINT CLEAR MEASURING CUPS
- WATER
- TEASPOON

THE METHOD

1. Pour a glass of juice and take a few sips to remind yourself of how strong it tastes.

2. Fill each of the measuring cups with 1 pint (16 fluid ounces) of water.

3. Measure out 1 teaspoon of juice and add it to one of the pints of water, stirring the mixture with the teaspoon.

4. Now take 1 teaspoon of liquid from that first measuring cup and add it to the second measuring cup, stirring it in again.

5. Repeat the process by adding 1 teaspoon of liquid from the second measuring cup to the third measuring cup.

6. Give the third cup a stir and sip a spoonful of it. Now take another sip from your glass of juice and compare.

7. How does it taste now? Just think: The third measuring cup had the same concentration of juice (1 ppm) that alerts a shark to the presence of blood!

ATM
OUT OF ORDER
CASH ONLY
GAS
SCHOOL
SCHOOL BUS

07

CHANCES OF SURVIVAL: SLIM TO NONE

SURVIVAL STRATEGIES: RATIOS AND PROPORTIONS; UNIT RATE

DEATH BY: SCORCHING SUN

THE DESERT DECISION

THE CHALLENGE

You're on a camping trip, driving from Los Angeles to Lake Havasu City in Arizona in an old school bus. After you leave Barstow, you enter the Mojave National Preserve, one of the hottest and driest places on Earth. It's desert country out here: Everywhere you look, all you see is sand, cactus, and an occasional jackrabbit making its way across the highway. The road is pretty empty.

After about an hour of driving, you see a sign: LAST GAS STATION FOR 200 MILES. The bus driver looks a bit worried as he pulls into the station. Why? Because he's read the sign that says: CASH ONLY. NO CREDIT CARDS ACCEPTED. Even more troublesome is the other sign over the ATM machine that reads: OUT OF ORDER.

The bus driver has only $2 in his wallet. You and your classmates check your pockets, but your grand total, including the bus driver's $2, is $23.63. Gas costs $2.78 a gallon in these parts. Your gas tank says you've only got $\frac{1}{8}$ of a tank of gas left. The driver tells you that the bus gets 17 miles to the gallon and that a full tank of gas is exactly 30 gallons.

If you use the $23.63 on gas, will that be enough to get you to the next gas station? Or will your bus wind up out of gas and bake in the scorching desert sun? Exactly how far will you be able to travel once you purchase the gas?

EUCLID'S ADVICE

Write down everything you know:

- **The bus has $\frac{1}{8}$ of a tank of gas left; a full tank can hold 30 gallons.**
- **You have $23.63 total.**
- **1 gallon of gas costs $2.78.**
- **The bus gets 17 miles to the gallon.**
- **You have 200 miles to go until you reach the next gas station.**

WORKSHEET

THE SOLUTION

YES! YOU CAN MAKE IT! YOU CAN TRAVEL 208.25 MILES WITH THE 12.25 GALLONS OF GAS YOU ALREADY HAD AND WERE ABLE TO PURCHASE.

Solve it, step-by-step:

1. First, you need to figure out how much gas is left in the tank. You have $\frac{1}{8}$ of a tank left. Let's rename $\frac{1}{8}$ to its decimal equivalent:

$$\frac{1}{8} = 1 \div 8 = 0.125$$

If a full tank can hold 30 gallons, and you have 0.125 of that amount left, multiply to get your answer.

$$30 \times 0.125 = 3.75 \text{ gallons}$$

That means the bus's gas tank has only 3.75 gallons of gas left.

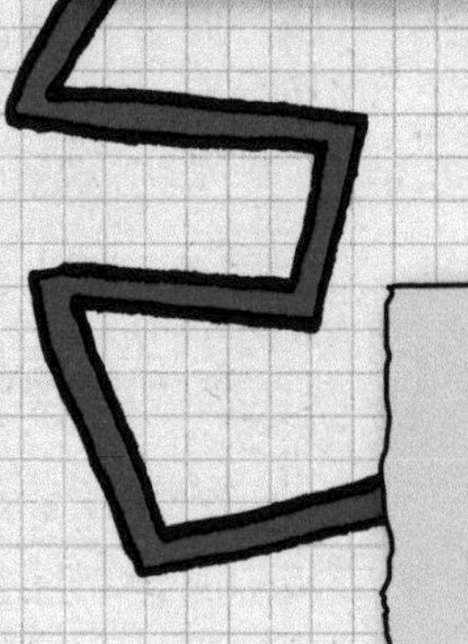

2. Now figure out how many gallons of gas \$23.63 will get you. To do this, divide your total amount of money (\$23.63) by the cost per gallon (\$2.78).

$$23.63 \div 2.78 = 8.5 \text{ gallons}$$

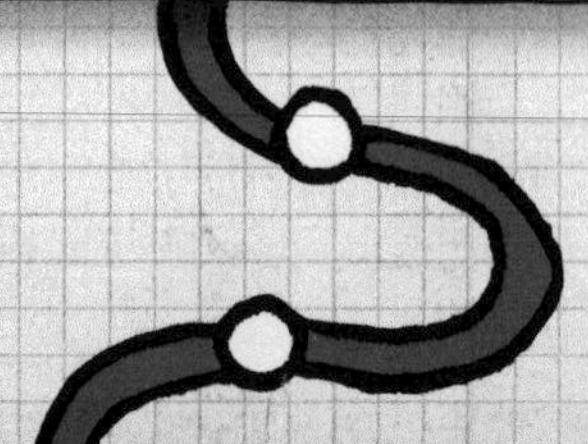

3. Now add up the total amount of gas you will have, based on your calculations in steps 1 and 2.

$$3.75 + 8.5 = 12.25 \text{ gallons}$$

4. Will 12.25 gallons of gas be enough to get you to the next gas station, 200 miles away? Figure out how many miles you can travel by multiplying the amount of gas you have (12.25 gallons) by the number of miles you can travel with each gallon (17 miles).

$$12.25 \times 17 = 208.25 \text{ miles}$$

You'll make it with 8.25 miles to spare!

MATH LAB

You can do some of your own gas-distance calculations, although they don't have to be perilous. All you have to do is get some information about any car's gas mileage (either your family car or one you've researched on the Internet) and the price of gas in your area. You can make the calculations even more interesting if you can find a road map with a clear indication of its scale (how many miles to the inch).

YOU WILL NEED

- OWNER'S MANUAL FOR YOUR FAMILY CAR OR A COMPUTER TO RESEARCH ANY CAR'S GAS MILEAGE
- PENCIL
- PAPER
- CALCULATOR
- ROAD MAP INCLUDING YOUR AREA

THE METHOD

1. Ask your parents how much they expect to pay (per gallon) when they buy gas, or note the price next time you're at a local gas station, or research it online.

2. Check the owner's manual, or research online, to find out how many gallons the car's fuel tank can hold and how many miles it can travel per gallon (on the highway).

3. Write those two figures down.

4. Using your calculator, figure out how much it would cost to fill the tank.

5. Now work out how far that tank full of gas would take you.

6. Look at the road map and find a destination that is about 150 miles from your home. Can you work out how many gallons of gas you'd need to get there, and how much it would cost?

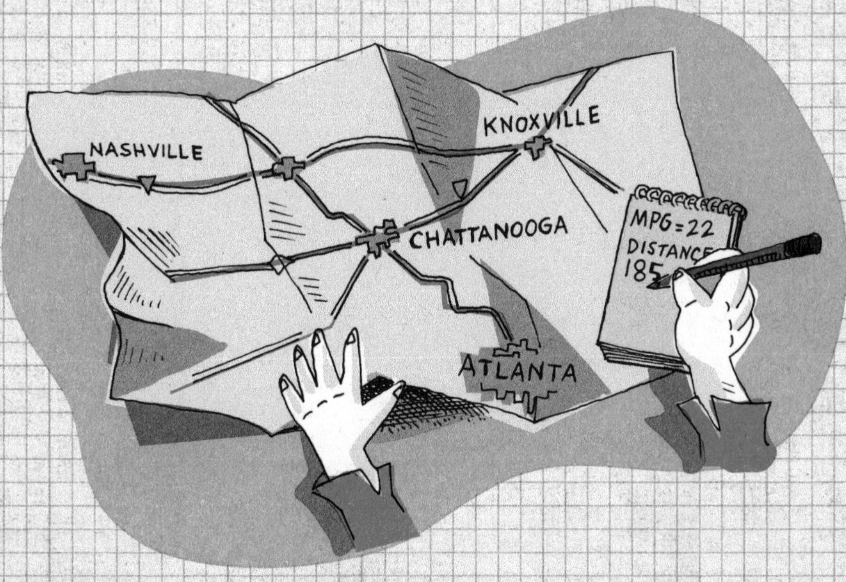

7. Bonus challenge: Find a vacation destination that you can reach if you set aside $100 for gas (don't forget that you have to drive back!).

THE SOLUTION: TO FIND HOW MUCH IT COSTS TO FILL THE TANK WITH GAS, MULTIPLY THE TANK'S SIZE BY THE PRICE OF GAS. TO FIND OUT HOW FAR A FULL TANK OF GAS WILL TAKE YOU, MULTIPLY THE SIZE OF THE TANK BY HOW MANY MILES THE CAR CAN TRAVEL PER GALLON.

THE DISAPPEARING DOLLAR

hree friends have a meal in a restaurant and they re charged $25. They each chip in with a $10 bill nd hand it to the waiter. The waiter, though, isn't ery good at math (like dividing the $5 change by 3), o he keeps $2 as a tip and hands each friend $1.

Everyone seems pretty happy with the deal until one of the friends starts thinking about it. The three of them paid $10 each but got $1 back, so that meant that they spent $9 each. And since there were three of them, the total was 3 × $9, or $27, plus the $2 tip for the waiter. That takes the total to $29.

What happened to the missing dollar?

TRICKY LANGUAGE

This mystery is an excellent example of why it is important to read things carefully—in math and in other subjects. The trick here are the words "plus the $2 tip for the waiter." Instead of adding the $2 ("*plus* the $2 tip"), you should *subtract* it.

Think about it. Subtract that $2 and you get $25, which is the amount the restaurant got. Each friend got $1 and the waiter got $2.

Another way of thinking about it is to remember that the friends also shared the cost of the $2 tip ($0.67 each). So they paid $9 for their share of the meal *and* their share of the tip. The food itself cost each friend $8.33, then the $0.67 tip took that to $9. So if each paid $10 and got $1 back, then everything really *does* work out.

DRINKING
WATER

08

CHANCES OF SURVIVAL: SLIM TO NONE

SURVIVAL STRATEGIES: RATIOS AND PROPORTIONS; UNIT RATE

DEATH BY: DEHYDRATION

THE CHALLENGE

It's 1851. You were on a whaling mission, but a terrible storm tore your ship apart. Out of a crew of 27, there are only 5 of you left, stranded on a rowboat waiting—hoping—to drift toward land or get picked up by a passing ship.

All you have to eat is a box full of cookies—20 in all. And, thankfully, a 40-gallon barrel marked "Drinking Water." Chained to that barrel is a metal measuring cup marked "1 cup." The first mate, the only officer left alive, remarked that he had heard that a 40-gallon barrel of water had lasted 10 men for 16 days after their ship, the SS *Jefferson*, went down several years ago.

You know you must establish hard-and-fast rules now about how much water each person can drink each day before everyone becomes crazy with thirst. The oceans abound with tales of what happens to dehydrated sailors. You don't want to end up like *those* people!

How long will the barrel of water keep the 5 of you alive until you either reach land or get rescued at sea? How many cups of water can each person drink each day? And, based on how many days you can survive with the available water supply, how can you divide the cookies between you so that each person gets a piece every day?

EUCLID'S ADVICE

Write down everything you know:

- **The barrel contains 40 gallons of water.**
- **A 40-gallon barrel kept 10 men alive for 16 days.**
- **There are 5 of you.**
- **A 1-cup measuring cup hangs on the barrel.**
- **You have 20 cookies.**

HINT: 1 gallon = 4 quarts

1 quart = 4 cups

WORKSHEET

THE SOLUTION

THE BARREL OF WATER WILL LAST FOR 32 DAYS. EACH PERSON CAN DRINK 4 CUPS OF WATER EACH DAY. EACH PERSON CAN EAT $\frac{1}{8}$ OF A COOKIE EACH DAY.

Solve it, step-by-step:

1. First, figure out how many gallons of water were consumed each day by the 10 men on the SS *Jefferson*. Divide the number of gallons of water (40 gallons) by the number of days the water lasted (16 days).

$$40 \div 16 = 2\frac{1}{2}$$

That means that an average of $2\frac{1}{2}$ gallons of water were consumed each day by the 10 people combined on the SS *Jefferson*.

2. Next, figure out how much water was consumed by each man on the SS *Jefferson* per day. Divide the $2\frac{1}{2}$ gallons of water among the 10 men.

$2\frac{1}{2} \div 10 =$

(rename the $2\frac{1}{2}$ as $\frac{5}{2}$) $\frac{5}{2} \div 10 =$

$\frac{5}{2} \div \frac{10}{1} =$

(think of a division as its related multiplication problem) $\frac{5}{2} \times \frac{1}{10} =$

(multiply the numerators and the denominators) $\frac{5}{20} =$

(rename the fraction in its simplest form) $\frac{1}{4}$

That means each man consumed $\frac{1}{4}$ gallon of water a day for 16 days. Since $\frac{1}{4}$ gallon a day was enough to keep the sailors on the *Jefferson* alive, it should be enough to keep you alive now, too.

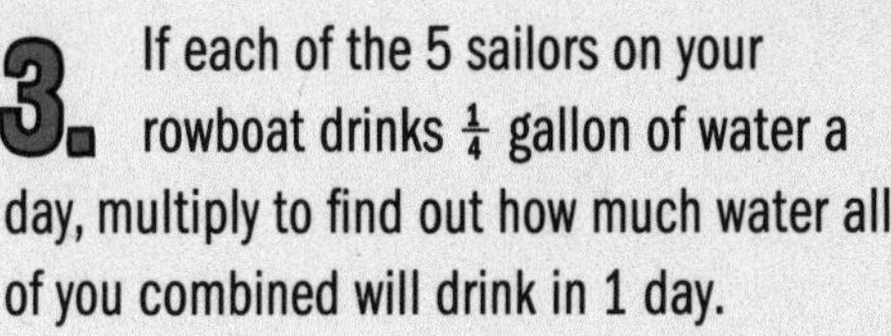

3. If each of the 5 sailors on your rowboat drinks $\frac{1}{4}$ gallon of water a day, multiply to find out how much water all of you combined will drink in 1 day.

$$5 \times \frac{1}{4} = \frac{5}{4} = 1\frac{1}{4}$$

That means $1\frac{1}{4}$ gallons of water total will be consumed on your rowboat daily.

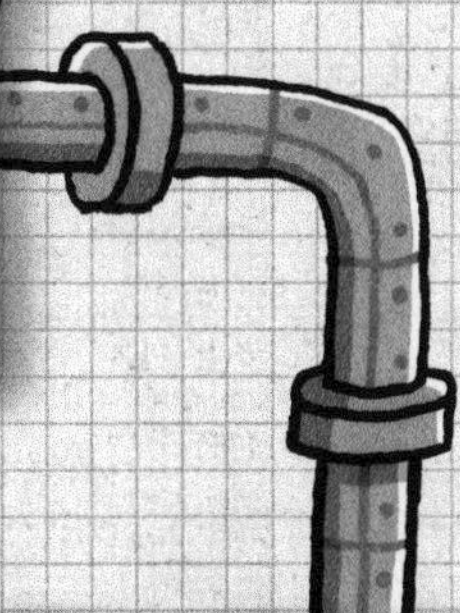

4. Divide the total amount of water (40 gallons) by the amount of water consumed each day ($1\frac{1}{4}$ gallons) to find out how long the water will last.

	$40 \div 1\frac{1}{4} =$
(rename the $1\frac{1}{4}$ as $\frac{5}{4}$)	$40 \div \frac{5}{4} =$
	$\frac{40}{1} \div \frac{5}{4} =$
(think of a division as its related multiplication problem)	$\frac{40}{1} \times \frac{4}{5} =$
(multiply the numerators and the denominators)	$\frac{160}{5} =$
(rename the fraction in its simplest form)	32

That means the water will last your crew 32 days.

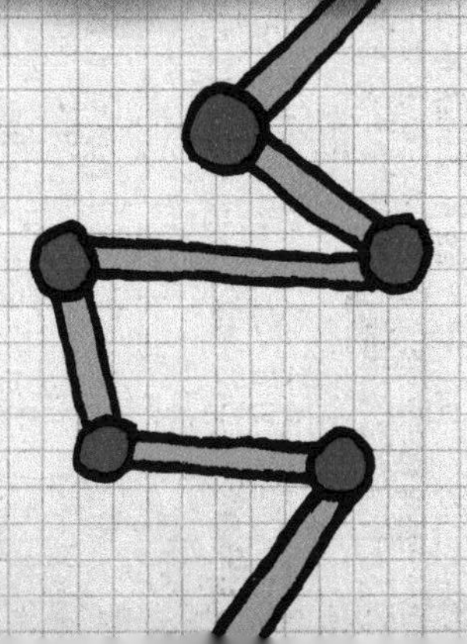

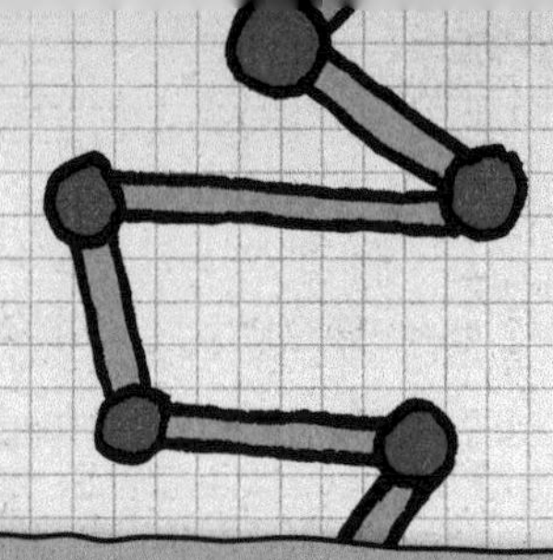

5. We know that the 40-gallon barrel of water will last the 5 sailors 32 days. Since the measuring cup attached to the barrel measures volume in cups, we need to convert *gallons* to cups to figure out how to ration the water equally among the 5 sailors.

First, convert $1\frac{1}{4}$ gallons to quarts. Remember, there are 4 quarts in 1 gallon. Since we're converting a larger unit to a smaller unit, multiply to get the answer:

$$1\frac{1}{4} \times 4 = \frac{5}{4} \times 4 = \frac{20}{4} = 5 \text{ quarts}$$

Second, convert 5 quarts to cups. Remember, there are 4 cups in 1 quart. Again, use multiplication to convert a larger unit to a smaller unit:

$$5 \times 4 = 20 \text{ cups}$$

That means $1\frac{1}{4}$ gallons = 20 cups, so the 5 men will split 20 cups of water a day.

Finally, divide 20 cups by the 5 men to find out how many cups each man can drink a day.

$$20 \div 5 = 4 \text{ cups}$$

In other words, each of the 5 men can drink 4 cups of water a day for 32 days before the water runs out.

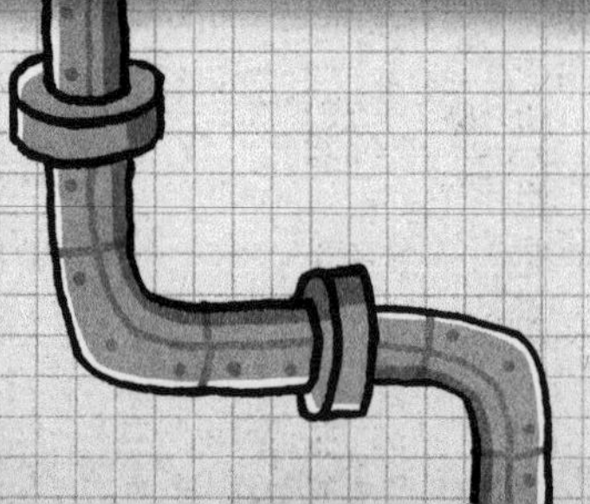

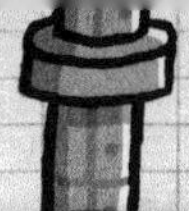

6. And what about those cookies? You know that you have enough water to hold out for 32 days. You have 20 cookies.

First, divide the number of number of cookies you have (20) by the number of days you can survive with your water supply (32) to find out how many pieces of cookie all of you can share each day.

$$20 \div 32 = \frac{20}{32} = \frac{5}{8} \text{ piece of cookie}$$

That means the 5 sailors can split $\frac{5}{8}$ of a cookie every day.

Next, divide the pieces of cookie that can be shared in one day ($\frac{5}{8}$) by the number of sailors (5) to find out how many pieces of cookie each sailor can have in a day.

$\frac{5}{8} \div 5 =$

$\frac{5}{8} \div \frac{5}{1} =$

(think of a division as its related multiplication problem) $\frac{5}{8} \times \frac{1}{5} =$

(multiply the numerators and the denominators) $\frac{5}{40} =$

(rename the fraction in its simplest form) $\frac{1}{8}$

That means that each of the 5 sailors can eat $\frac{1}{8}$ of a cookie a day for 32 days!

MATH LAB

It's important to be able to mix large measurements with small ones in order to finish calculations like the one in this challenge. You're lucky not to be shipwrecked or lost at sea on a drifting ship, but you might need to work out portions of food for lots of people.

This tasty demonstration gives you a chance to work out something almost as important: How much ice cream to feed the guests at your next birthday party. One of the best parts of this lab is that you have to buy some ice cream to do the testing. Can you manage it?

YOU WILL NEED

- ONE $\frac{1}{2}$-GALLON CONTAINER OF ICE CREAM
- ICE-CREAM SCOOP
- MEASURING CUP (HOLDS AT LEAST 1 CUP)

THE METHOD

1. Assume that you will be serving ice cream cones at your party, and that each cone will have one scoop.

2. Take a cone-sized scoop of ice cream and plop it into the measuring cup.

3. Continue scooping ice cream into the measuring cup—and counting each scoop—until the ice cream is level with the 1-cup line.

4. Pack the ice cream down and add another scoop or two if there are gaps between the scoops inside the measuring cup.

5. Record how many scoops you needed to hit the 1-cup line.

6. Using this information, how could you find the number of scoops in a $\frac{1}{2}$-gallon container?

THE SOLUTION: SINCE THERE ARE 16 CUPS IN A GALLON, THAT MEANS THERE ARE 8 CUPS IN A $\frac{1}{2}$ GALLON. MULTIPLY THE NUMBER OF SCOOPS BY 8 TO FIND OUT HOW MANY SCOOPS ARE IN A $\frac{1}{2}$-GALLON CONTAINER.

LORDZ
GRAFFITI
KEEP OUT
DANGER

09

CHANCES OF SURVIVAL: SLIM TO NONE

SURVIVAL STRATEGIES: MAKE USE OF STRUCTURE

DEATH BY: DEMOLITION

THE CHALLENGE

Your friend Juan was in the wrong place at the wrong time: Bank robbers have taken him hostage and locked him *somewhere* in an apartment building that is going to be demolished in 30 minutes. The bank robbers have fled with their loot, so you can begin looking for him, but where should you start?

There are 11 floors in the apartment building, and at least 10 empty apartments on each floor. You try the ground floor first. Wait—you see a piece of paper in one of the old mail slots! You grab it and read:

10 · 7 · 14 · 18 11 3 · 15
4 · 7 · 10 · 11 · 16 · 6 22 · 10 · 7
21 · 7 · 24 · 7 · 16 · 22 · 10 6 · 17 · 17 · 20
17 · 16 22 · 10 · 7 21 · 7 · 24 · 7 · 16 · 22 · 10
8 · 14 · 17 · 17 · 20

»12 · 23 · 3 · 16

It's a coded message! You're sure of that because Juan is obsessed with Edgar Allan Poe stories, especially "The Gold Bug," which features a coded message. And—yes! The last 4 numbers must represent Juan's name. What else do you remember from that story? Well, you can use patterns to help decode the message.

He must have come up with a pattern for these numbers. If 12 = J, 23 = U, 3 = A, and 16 = N, can you figure out the pattern, crack the code, and help rescue Juan before it's too late?

EUCLID'S ADVICE

Start by creating a "key" on the worksheet, writing down what each letter in the code represents:

- **We know that the last word "12 · 23 · 3 · 16" represents Juan's name, so add these conclusions to your "key":**

12 = J, 23 = U, 3 = A, 16 = N

- **Next, follow Poe's advice and find the pattern to crack the code. What do you notice? The letters in the beginning of the alphabet have lower numbers than those toward the end. Do you see a pattern developing that you can work with?**

HINT: Write out the entire alphabet, plugging in the numbers you know.

WORKSHEET

THE SOLUTION

THE MESSAGE READS:

HELP I AM
BEHIND THE SEVENTH DOOR
ON THE SEVENTH FLOOR
—JUAN

Solve it, step-by-step:

1. The original message looked like this:

10 · 7 · 14 · 18   11   3 · 15
4 · 7 · 10 · 11 · 16 · 6   22 · 10 · 7
21 · 7 · 24 · 7 · 16 · 22 · 10   6 · 17 · 17 · 20
17 · 16   22 · 10 · 7   21 · 7 · 24 · 7 · 16 · 22 · 10
8 · 14 · 17 · 17 · 20

»12 · 23 · 3 · 16

2. When you replaced these four numbers in this way

12 = J, 23 = U, 3 = A, 16 = N

the message became:

10 · 7 · 14 · 18   11   A · 15
4 · 7 · 10 · 11 · N · 6   22 · 10 · 7
21 · 7 · 24 · 7 · N · 22 · 10   6 · 17 · 17 · 20
17 · N   22 · 10 · 7   21 · 7 · 24 · 7 · N · 2 · 10
8 · 14 · 17 · 17 · 20

»JUAN

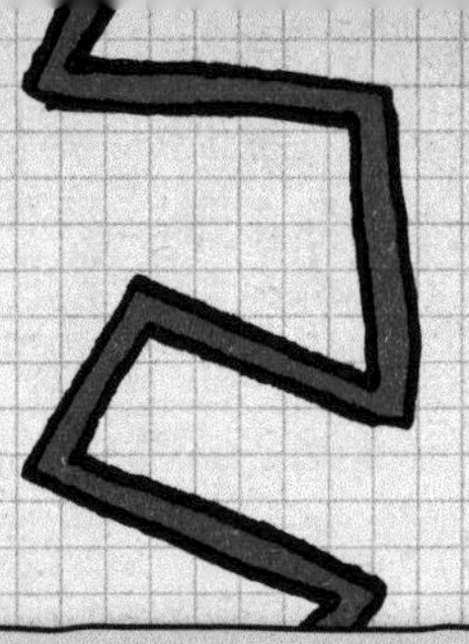

3. Next, write out the entire alphabet and assign each letter the number in which it occurs in the alphabet. This is a good place to start. Next, plug in numbers for the letters you do know, and try to figure out the pattern.

A	1	3
B	2	
C	3	
D	4	
E	5	
F	6	
G	7	
H	8	
I	9	
J	10	12
K	11	
L	12	
M	13	

N	14	16
O	15	
P	16	
Q	17	
R	18	
S	19	
T	20	
U	21	23
V	22	
W	23	
X	24	
Y	25	
Z	26	

4. Do you see the pattern emerging? The letters are assigned numerical values two more than their placement in the alphabet. So, A is letter 1 in the alphabet and Juan gave it the value "3."

$$1 + 2 = 3$$

You can find the value of B by taking its placement in the alphabet (2) and adding 2.

$$2 + 2 = 4$$

Fill in the rest of the chart to crack the code.

A	**1**	3
B	**2**	4
C	**3**	5
D	**4**	6
E	**5**	7
F	**6**	8
G	**7**	9
H	**8**	10
I	**9**	11
J	**10**	12
K	**11**	13
L	**12**	14
M	**13**	15

N	**14**	16
O	**15**	17
P	**16**	18
Q	**17**	19
R	**18**	20
S	**19**	21
T	**20**	22
U	**21**	23
V	**22**	24
W	**23**	25
X	**24**	26
Y	**25**	1
Z	**26**	2

The note reads:

Help I am
behind the seventh door
on the seventh floor
—Juan

MATH LAB

You don't have to be kidnapped to write a message in a secret code. You could be, for instance, telling people how and where to find some hidden treasure.

Why not hide some treasure—a candy bar or two, for example—and set your friends the task of finding it from your coded instructions. You can use letters, numbers, or a combination of both to work out your code, but remember two things:

- You must always use the same symbols to stand for the same letters.
- Don't lose the key to your code!

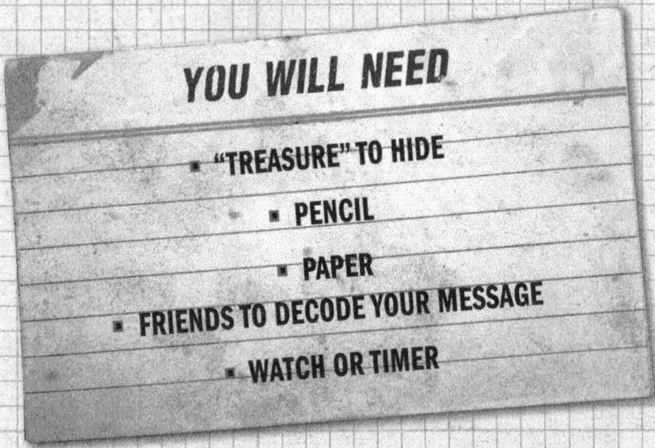

THE METHOD

1. First, hide the "treasure" somewhere that your friends can reach if they crack the code—in a particular drawer, behind a tree, or under a hat.

2. Now set up a code that uses a different symbol (another letter or a number) to stand for each of the 26 letters in the alphabet.

3. Write out each of the "normal" letters down a column on your paper.

4. Write out the "code" equivalents of each letter beside each letter.

5. On a separate sheet, write out the instructions for your friends using this code. For their sake, don't make the message too short. Otherwise, they might find it harder to find patterns (such as seeing how many times certain letters or numbers pop up). You can help them crack the code if you end your message with your name written in code as Juan did.

6. Give them a certain amount of time—say 10 minutes—to work out the code and find the treasure.

A5
THE ALPS

10

CHANCES OF SURVIVAL: SLIM TO NONE

SURVIVAL STRATEGIES: RATIOS AND PROPORTIONS

DEATH BY: RIVAL SPY

QUICK CHANGE ON THE TRAIN

THE CHALLENGE

It's December 31, 1893, and everyone on the famous Orient Express train is in high spirits as they prepare for New Year's celebrations. You left Paris before sunrise and have traveled 6 hours across France. In that time the famous train has covered 360 miles, speeding smoothly toward the Alps. Soon you'll enter the 2-mile-long

THE ORIENT EXPRESS

The Orient Express was a luxurious, high-speed train that operated from 1883 to 2009. It originally traveled across Europe from Paris to Istanbul in Turkey. Along the way it passed spectacular scenery and stopped at many of Europe's most beautiful cities. Because of its top-class speed, comfort, and service, the Orient Express gained a reputation as a magnet for the rich, powerful, and the mysterious.

Courcheval Tunnel, and the train will be plunged into darkness.

But you're in no position to sit back and enjoy the ride. You have a document that will bring Ivan Renkovic, an international war criminal, to justice, which you'll hand over at the Swiss border crossing, about 3 miles beyond the tunnel.

But Renkovic has spies everywhere, and they will kill in order to get that document. In fact, you just overheard a man in the next car, dressed like a conductor, asking whether someone with your description was on the train. You need to figure out a way to get past him to the part of the train he's already searched.

You duck out of the corridor and find yourself in the closet with the dining car supplies, including chef uniforms. Wait! If you could change clothes it might help you get past him. And no one would stop to ask a chef for a ticket!

You look around and assemble an outfit, though there's no room to change. Shirt, hat, pants, white socks, white shoes, black belt, necktie. But you'd really need to be back out in the corridor to get all this on. You will need 2 minutes with no one looking. Then everything goes dark. You're in the tunnel!

How long will the train be in the tunnel? Is there enough time to change into the chef's outfit while the train is in the tunnel?

VARIABLES

A variable is one of the most useful tools in math. It stands in place of a quantity and is usually represented by a letter, like *a* or *x*. It can be a value that you are trying to figure out or solving for, as in a linear equation: $x + 3 = 5$, where $x = 2$. Or, it can be a value you know and need to plug into a formula to get the desired answer, like in the area of a rectangle: $A = l \times w$, where you plug in the length (l) and width (w) to solve for the area (A).

EUCLID'S ADVICE

Write down everything you know:

- **The train has traveled 360 miles in 6 hours.**
- **The Courcheval Tunnel is 2 miles long.**
- **The sudden darkness means you've entered the tunnel.**
- **You need 2 minutes to change, and you need the train to be in the tunnel, hidden in darkness, for that whole time.**
- **Proportional ratios will help you solve this problem.**

WORKSHEET

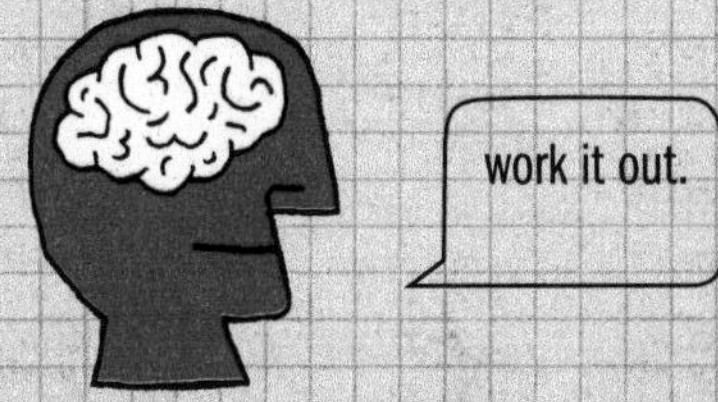
work it out.

THE SOLUTION

THE TRAIN WILL TAKE 2 MINUTES TO TRAVEL THROUGH THE TUNNEL. YOU WILL HAVE JUST ENOUGH TIME TO CHANGE!

Solve it, step-by-step:

1. To find out how long the train will be in the tunnel, you first need to determine the speed of the train. You already know the length of the tunnel (2 miles). You can figure out your speed by dividing the distance you've traveled by the time it has taken so far:

$$360 \text{ miles} \div 6 \text{ hours} = 60 \text{ miles/hour}$$

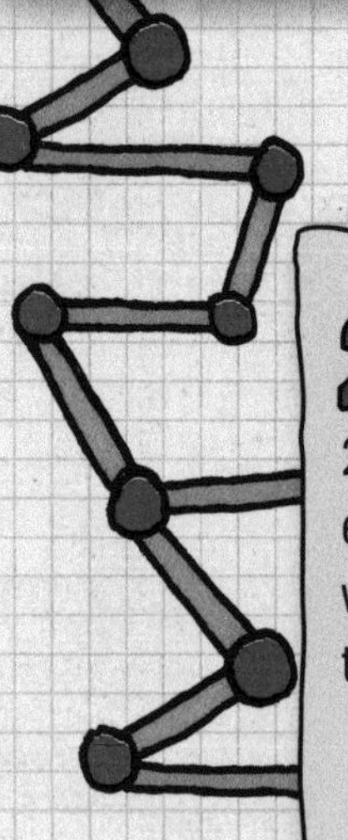

2. Now you know you can travel 60 miles in 1 hour. But you only need to travel 2 miles. How long will that take you? Set up an equation using two proportional ratios and the variable *t* to figure out how long you will be in the tunnel.

$$\frac{60}{1} = \frac{2}{t}$$

$$60t = 2$$

$$t = \frac{1}{30}$$

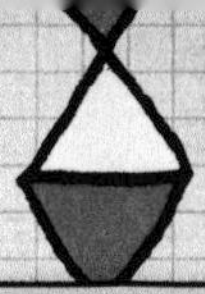

3. What does $\frac{1}{30}$ represent? The number of hours that you'll be in the tunnel. In other words, $\frac{1}{30}$ of 60 minutes. Multiply to get the answer as a number of minutes.

$$\frac{1}{30} \times 60 = \frac{60}{30} = 2 \text{ minutes}$$

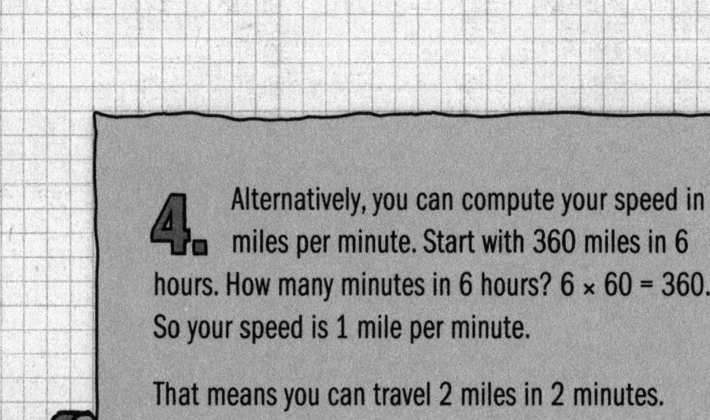

4. Alternatively, you can compute your speed in miles per minute. Start with 360 miles in 6 hours. How many minutes in 6 hours? 6 × 60 = 360. So your speed is 1 mile per minute.

That means you can travel 2 miles in 2 minutes.

You have *just* enough time to change!

MATH LAB

You can better understand the difficulties of this challenge by trying to do a version of it at home. Get some friends to come over and make a contest out of it. You'll try to re-create some of the conditions of the train, and that means trying to do some of the activity in the dark. So, it would be best to do this after dark or in a room that you can darken completely with curtains and blinds.

YOU WILL NEED

- WATCH OR OTHER TIMER
- SMALL FLASHLIGHT
- ASSORTMENT OF LOOSE-FITTING CLOTHING, SUCH AS:
  - SHIRT
  - JACKET
  - NECKTIE (NOT CLIP-ON)
  - SKIRT
  - SOCKS

THE METHOD

1. Have someone time each person's turn. That person should have a timer they can see in the dark or a small flashlight to help them read it.

2. Assemble the loose-fitting spare clothes neatly on a chair, table, or counter.

3. Ask the first player to step up to the clothes.

4. At a given signal, the lights get turned off, the person with the watch starts timing 2 minutes, and the first player tries to quickly put on the spare outfit.

5. The person timing should yell "time" at 2 minutes, and the player should stop.

6. Turn on the lights and see how neatly the person managed to put on the new clothes.

7. Repeat steps 3 through 6 until everyone has had a turn.

8. Vote to see who put on the clothes most convincingly. Would the spy have seen through this disguise?

EUCLID

THE ADVENTURES OF

MARVIN THE MARVELOUS MATHEMATICIAN

ISSUE #1

11

CHANCES OF SURVIVAL: SLIM TO NONE

SURVIVAL STRATEGIES: EXPRESSIONS AND EQUATIONS

DEATH BY: DISAPPOINTMENT

BUYING A PYRAMID

THE CHALLENGE

You can't believe your luck. Your local comic book store *finally* has the extremely rare first issue of *The Adventures of Marvin the Marvelous Mathematician*. But it costs $400! It will take forever to earn that much money from your weekend job delivering newspapers to all 9,000 people in your town.

Your friend Trey promises that this "pyramid scheme" he's invested in will help you get the money—and fast. You just need to invest $100 to start, a sum that's taken you weeks to save. The pyramid scheme works like this: One person (call him "Top of the Pyramid") gets 10 people ("Layer 2") to pay him $100. Each of *them*, in turn, is told to find 10 *more* people ("Layer 3") to pay $100 each. So far, so good: If everyone has found recruits, then Top of the Pyramid has made his $1,000 and all of the Layer 2 people have made $900 ($1,000 minus the $100 they paid to Top of the Pyramid).

Trey tells you he's in Layer 4 of the pyramid. If you hand him the $100, then he figures you'll be making $900 in a matter of days.

If you participate in Layer 5 of this scheme, and you can only recruit people from your town, are there enough people in your 9,000-person town for you to make $900?

EUCLID'S ADVICE

Pyramid schemes got their name because of how they look if you worked out their operation in a diagram. They start out with one person (Top of the Pyramid) and then each layer gets bigger—like working down from the top of a real pyramid. Each person invests $100 and then must find 10 more people to pay that person, etc. A tree diagram can help you visualize the pyramid scheme as the layers continue.

WORKSHEET

THE SOLUTION

NO, YOUR TOWN'S POPULATION IS TOO SMALL IF YOU ARE IN LAYER 5.

Solve it, step-by-step:

1. If you start to draw a tree diagram demonstrating this pyramid scheme, you'll see that things start to get a little out of control from Layer 2 onward. Once the person at the top of the pyramid has made his or her money, the number of people that need to be involved starts to increase rapidly.

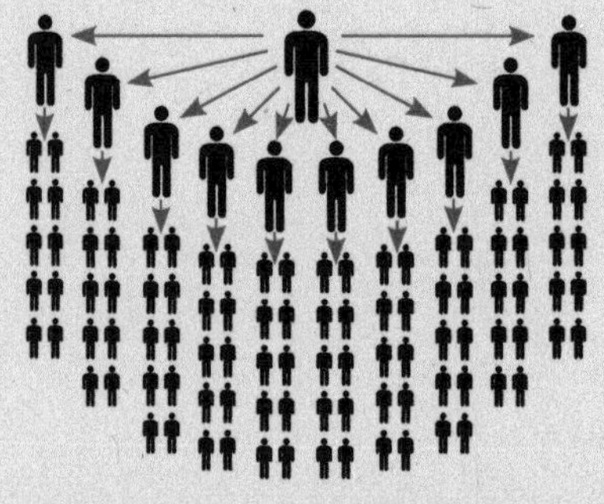

2. Think of it this way: If there are 10 people in Layer 2, and they each have to find 10 *more* people, how many people is that?

$$10 \times 10 = 100$$

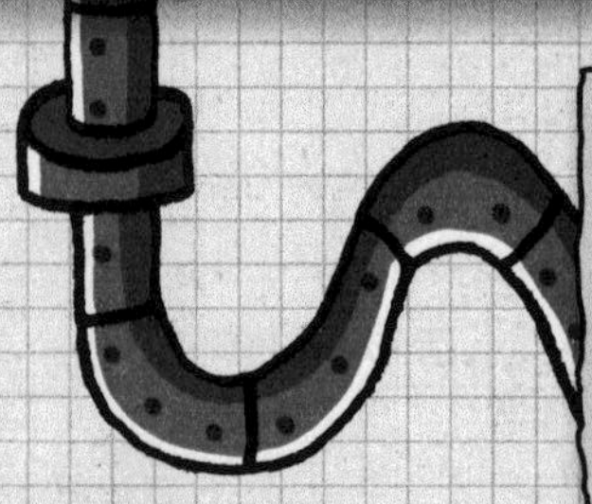

3. Now consider what that means for Layer 3: There are 100 people in this layer, and each of *them* must find 10 people.

$$100 \times 10 = 1,000$$

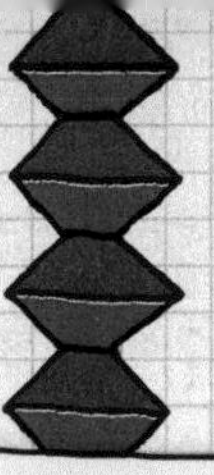

4. In Layer 4 there are 1,000 people, and each of them must find 10 people.

$$1{,}000 \times 10 = 10{,}000$$

5. Wow! That means by Layer 5, there won't be enough people in your 9,000-person town to participate in this scheme.

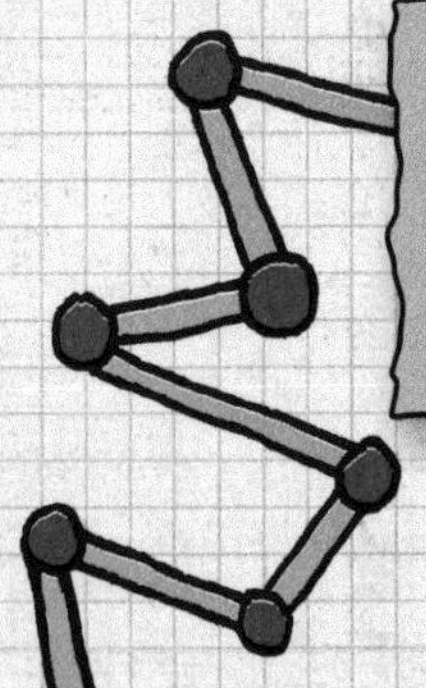

6. If the layers could continue, think of how quickly they'll grow to huge numbers of participants:

$$10{,}000 \times 10 = 100{,}000 \text{ for Layer 6}$$

$$100{,}000 \times 10 = 1{,}000{,}000 \text{ for Layer 7}$$

In other words, as the pyramid scheme continues, it gets harder and harder—and then impossible—to find new recruits. That means a few people (at the very top) might make a profit, but lots and lots of people who pay $100 at the bottom lose all of their investment and never get anything back. You certainly wouldn't make any money in Layer 5! It's definitely *not* a good idea to get involved. This is why pyramid schemes are often illegal.

MATH LAB

You can work up a mini pyramid scheme—showing how they soon fall apart—in your own classroom. Don't use real money, though!

YOU WILL NEED

- 25 SMALL SQUARES OF RECYCLED PAPER, MINIMUM
- 25 PLAYERS, MINIMUM

THE METHOD

1. Explain that you have a method of making everyone rich—in paper squares, anyway.
2. Settle on a value for each square: 1 square can be worth $100.
3. Distribute 1 square to each person.

4. You can be the Top of the Pyramid.

5. Ask 10 people to give you $100 (1 square) each, to get the ball rolling. You now have $1,000.

6. Get each of them to find 10 people to pay them $100. Other players may refuse if they want to.

7. Keep going until the players at the bottom of the pyramid are no longer able to find new players willing to pay the $100 entry fee.

8. How many people made money? How many people lost money?

9. Can you imagine other versions of this scheme (there are dozens of variations) that would make the first people richer—or allow the pyramid to operate longer? Try starting with more people at the top, with fewer people at the top, with larger entry fees, or with different numbers of recruits that each participant must find.

12

CHANCES OF SURVIVAL: SLIM TO NONE

SURVIVAL STRATEGIES: MAKE USE OF STRUCTURE

DEATH BY: SUFFOCATION

THE CHALLENGE

You're in an ancient Egyptian tomb. Phew! It's dark and the air feels so stale that Professor Aziz must be right: The secret sliding door hadn't opened for more than 3,500 years . . . until now . . . and it must have been really airtight. The professor has spent his entire career searching for this magnificent hidden tomb, which dates

EGYPT'S DYNASTIES

Historians divide ancient Egyptian history into 30 dynasties. A dynasty is a series of rulers (like the Egyptian pharaohs) belonging to the same family. The first (earliest) dynasty was about 5,000 years ago, when Egypt first became unified. The numbering continues through Egyptian history, including periods when foreign powers such as Persia ruled the country. Most historians consider the 30th dynasty to be the last, ending when Alexander the Great conquered Egypt in 332 B.C.

from ancient Egypt's 18th Dynasty. Only the professor and his two assistants, Nahid and you, know about this tomb, and you've made sure that no one else has followed you here.

Apart from the patch of light by the secret door, the only light comes from the flashlight you've carried with you, and you can't see how far the tomb extends. You put your camera down just inside the door (it's too dark for photos), and walk farther into the tomb. The walls are covered with hieroglyphics, and Professor Aziz stops to translate one or two as the three of you walk farther and farther into the unexplored tunnel.

Professor Aziz has stopped again. "This is a very long inscription. And it is in the form of a riddle, which the ancient Egyptians loved. Look—there's a picture of the door where we entered, with sunlight streaming in. See? And next to it is a series of sandals, which the Egyptians used to mean 'feet.' There's 1 sandal, then 3, then 6, then 10, then . . . let's see, 15 sandals. But here comes the riddle, which reads 'Add 3 more and then add all.'"

"What do you suppose it's talking about?" asks Nahid.

"Well, it's actually very simple. It's telling us where the other door is in relation to the entrance door," says the professor.

"You mean there's another secret door, leading—"

And at that moment, you hear a loud creaking sound and look back to see the door sliding shut. The three of you start back, hoping to reach it before it shuts completely, but in your rush you drop the flashlight. It flickers out and you can't get it to turn on again. The light ahead is getting fainter and fainter as the door shuts . . . and then blackness. Pitch dark.

The three of you find the wall and work your way slowly back to the door where you left your camera. When you find the camera, the wall above it seems no different from anywhere else along the passage. Pushing and pressing does nothing, and there's no way of pulling it. What can you do? That tomb was airtight—when will the air run out? No one knows you're here.

Your only hope is that riddle on the tomb wall. Use the pattern to decipher the riddle and figure out how many feet you are from the hidden exit door. Solve it and escape a deadly fate.

EUCLID'S ADVICE

Write down everything you know:

- **The riddle is the key. The sandals represent feet, so it must be telling you how many feet from the entrance door (which was pictured on the wall, don't forget) the exit door is.**
- **There seemed to be a pattern: 1, 3, 6, 10, and 15. Then it said "add 3 more."**
- **Finally, it said "then add all." Maybe that also has something to do with the pattern.**

WORKSHEET

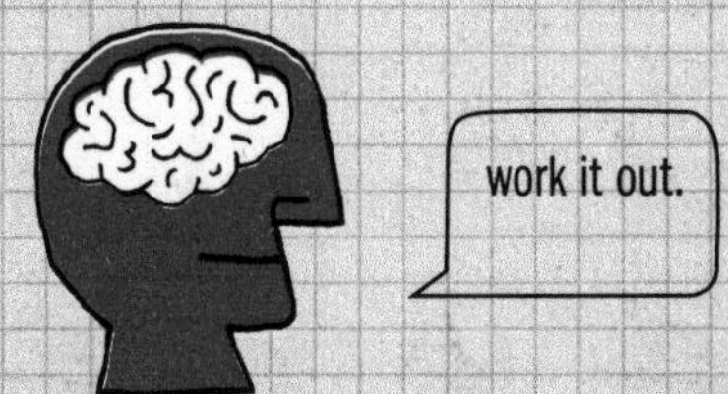
work it out.

THE SOLUTION

THE SECRET EXIT DOOR IS 120 FEET DOWN THE PASSAGE FROM THE ENTRANCE DOOR.

Solve it, step-by-step:

1. The key to the riddle is in the pattern formed by the numbers 1, 3, 6, 10, and 15. So, begin by figuring out how the pattern works:

The difference between 1 and 3 is 2.

The difference between 3 and 6 is 3.

The difference between 6 and 10 is 4.

The difference between 10 and 15 is 5.

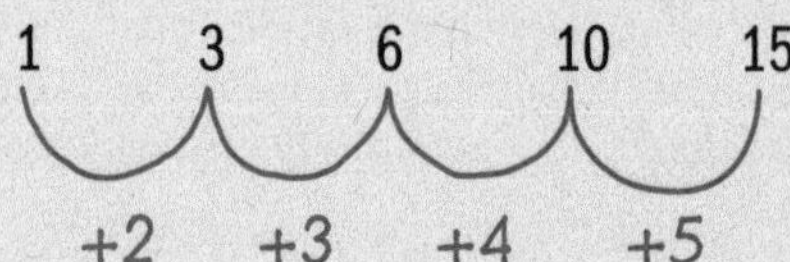

The number that represents the difference between each pair of numbers is increasing by 1 each time.

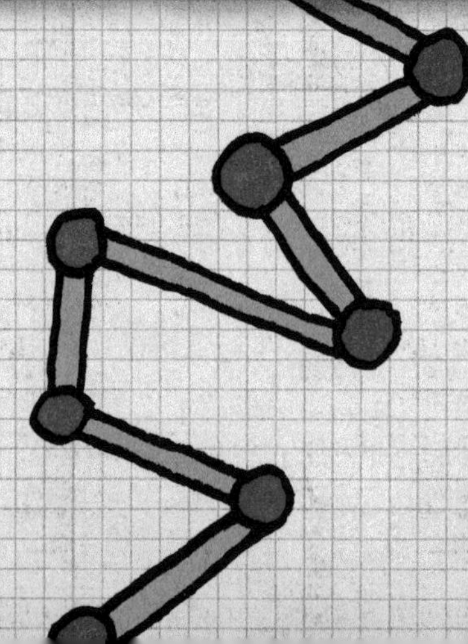

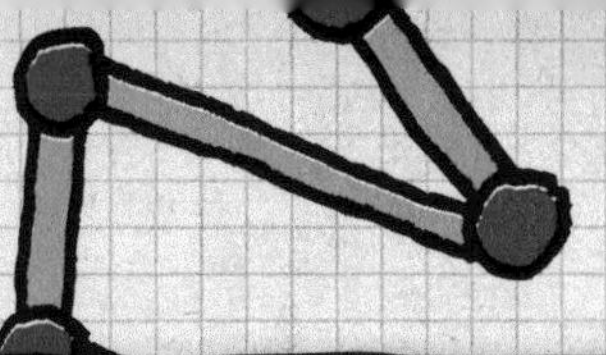

2. Now that you've discovered the pattern, "add 3 more" by extending the pattern 3 more times.

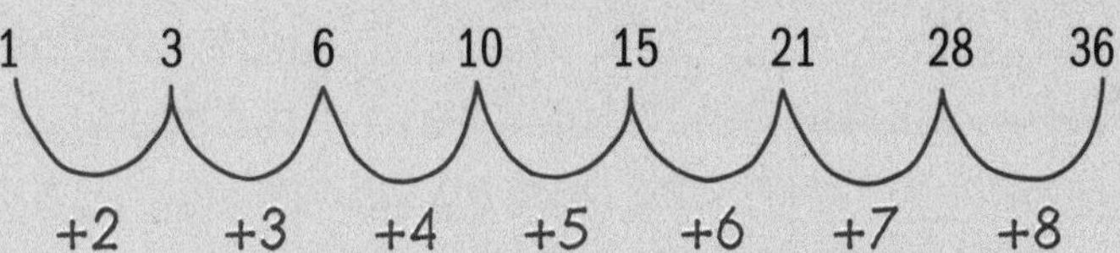

That means the pattern is now: 1, 3, 6, 10, 15, 21, 28, 36.

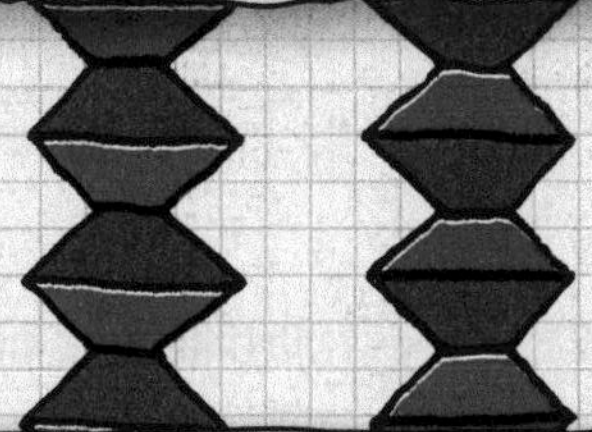

3. Next, you must "add all," which means you should add all of the numbers in the pattern:

$$1 + 3 + 6 + 10 + 15 + 21 + 28 + 36 = 120$$

That means the exit is 120 feet from the entrance!

MATH LAB

You can discover series of numbers all around you. One of the most common number series, which occurs frequently in nature, involves what are called Fibonacci numbers. They take their name from an Italian mathematician who lived about 800 years ago, in the city of Pisa (famous for its Leaning Tower). He devised the following number series:

0, 1, 1, 2, 3, 5, 8, 13, 21, 34 . . .

Can you see how this series develops? Each number in the series is the sum of the two preceding numbers—once you get going, that is. So the second "1" is the sum of 0 and 1; the 8 is the sum of 3 and 5; the 34 is the sum of 13 and 21, and so on.

That would be pretty interesting in itself, except people have since noticed that lots of things in nature are Fibonacci numbers. This activity is a neat way of getting you and some of your friends to be naturalists and mathematicians at the same time—on the hunt for more examples of the mysterious Fibonacci numbers.

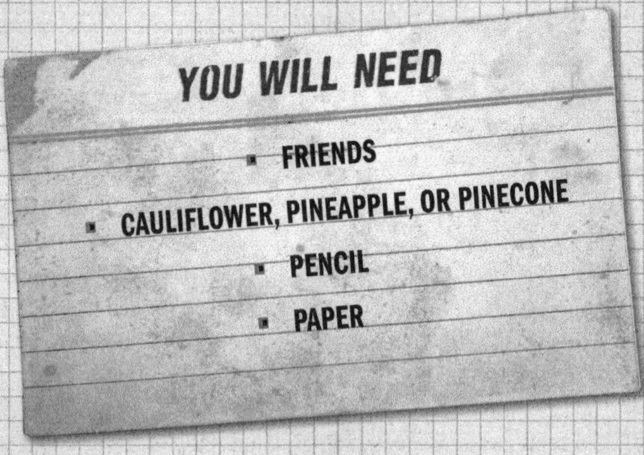

THE METHOD

1. Get one or more friends to help you do this investigation, which can last up to 1 week.

2. Explain about number series in general, and in particular how the Fibonacci series works.

3. If you have a cauliflower head, examine it from above until you can see the center of the flowers.

4. Trace and count out the number of spirals leading out from that center—first the clockwise spirals and then the counterclockwise spirals.

5. See whether each number falls in the Fibonacci sequence of numbers.

6. Try the same by tracing the spirals (each way) along the outside of a pineapple or pinecone.

7. Now see who can find the greatest number of Fibonacci numbers in nature, writing down those examples (and the numbers) over the course of 1 week.

You can look at the number of petals on flowers, leaf arrangements, the seeds in a horizontally sliced apple, seed heads—pretty much anything to do with plants. You can even challenge yourself to find examples from plant life where Fibonacci numbers are *not* found (e.g., 4, 6, 7)!

13 | **CHANCES OF SURVIVAL:** SLIM TO NONE
SURVIVAL STRATEGIES: ANALYTICAL THINKING
DEATH BY: ZOMBIES

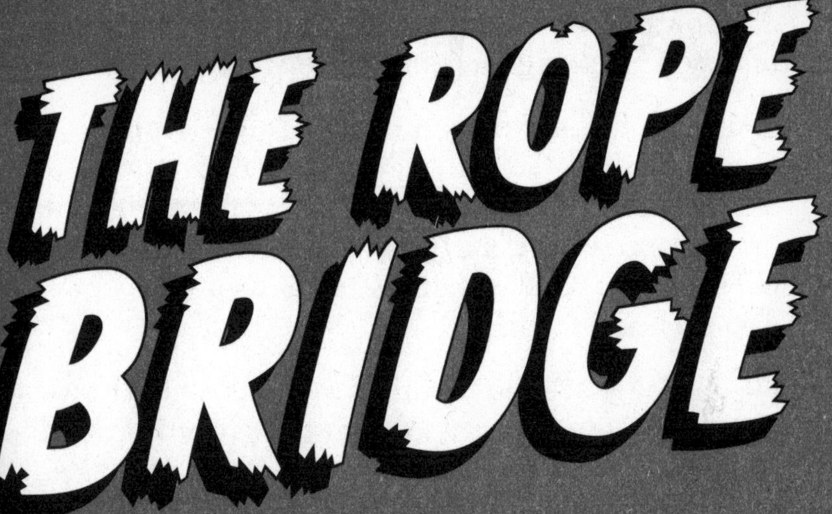

THE ROPE BRIDGE

THE CHALLENGE

Arnie, Bella, Carlos, and you are trapped in the Andes Mountains, being chased through Incan ruins by zombies. Your vacation could not have gone any worse.

The zombies are making their way up the mountain now—they're about 20 minutes away—and they obviously have a "take no prisoners" policy. You need to get away—and fast.

But how? You know that a local helicopter makes daily pickups at 6 P.M. exactly—but on the other side of a rope footbridge crossing a deep mountain gorge.

You go as fast as you can to the bridge—which is a swaying, rickety structure with a sheer drop of several thousand feet. Because it's now dark, and the bridge is so rickety, *and* you have only one flashlight between you, the flashlight is going to have to be carried back and forth.

You explain, "We can do this if we think logically. No more than 2 people can cross at the same time, and we know from gym class that some of us are faster than others. I figure that I can cross in 1 minute, Bella in 2 minutes, Carlos in 3 minutes, and Arnie in 8 minutes."

It's 5:44 P.M. You need to hustle if you're going to make it to the helicopter in time!

Can you determine how to get all 4 of you across the bridge, 2 at a time, in time for the 6 P.M. pickup, making sure that each person crossing can use the flashlight?

EUCLID'S ADVICE

Write down everything you know:

- **Before you start across the bridge, remember that someone must come back from the other side (with the flashlight) for each trip.**

HINT: Draw a picture to help you visualize each trip across the bridge.

WORKSHEET

THE SOLUTION

YOU CAN MAKE IT TO THE HELICOPTER PICKUP POINT IN 15 MINUTES WITH 1 MINUTE TO SPARE. THERE ARE TWO POSSIBLE SOLUTIONS.

Solve it, step-by-step:

YOU HAVE 16 MINUTES TO CROSS THE BRIDGE.

6:00 – 5:44 = 16 minutes

SOLUTION A:

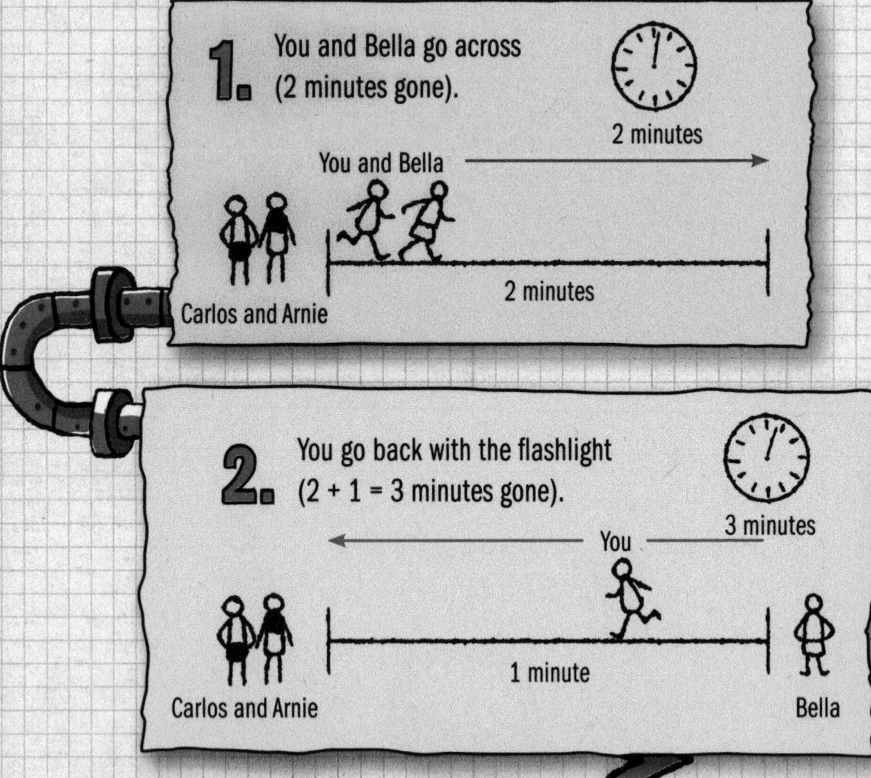

3. Carlos and Arnie go across, leaving you at the start (3 + 8 = 11 minutes gone).
11 minutes
Carlos and Arnie
8 minutes
You
Bella
4. Bella goes back to the start with the flashlight (11 + 2 = 13 minutes gone).
13 minutes
Bella
2 minutes
You
Carlos and Arnie
5. You and Bella make the final trip across (13 + 2 = 15 minutes gone).
15 minutes
You and Bella
2 minutes
Carlos and Arnie
6. You make the helicopter in 15 minutes with 1 minute to spare!

SOLUTION B:

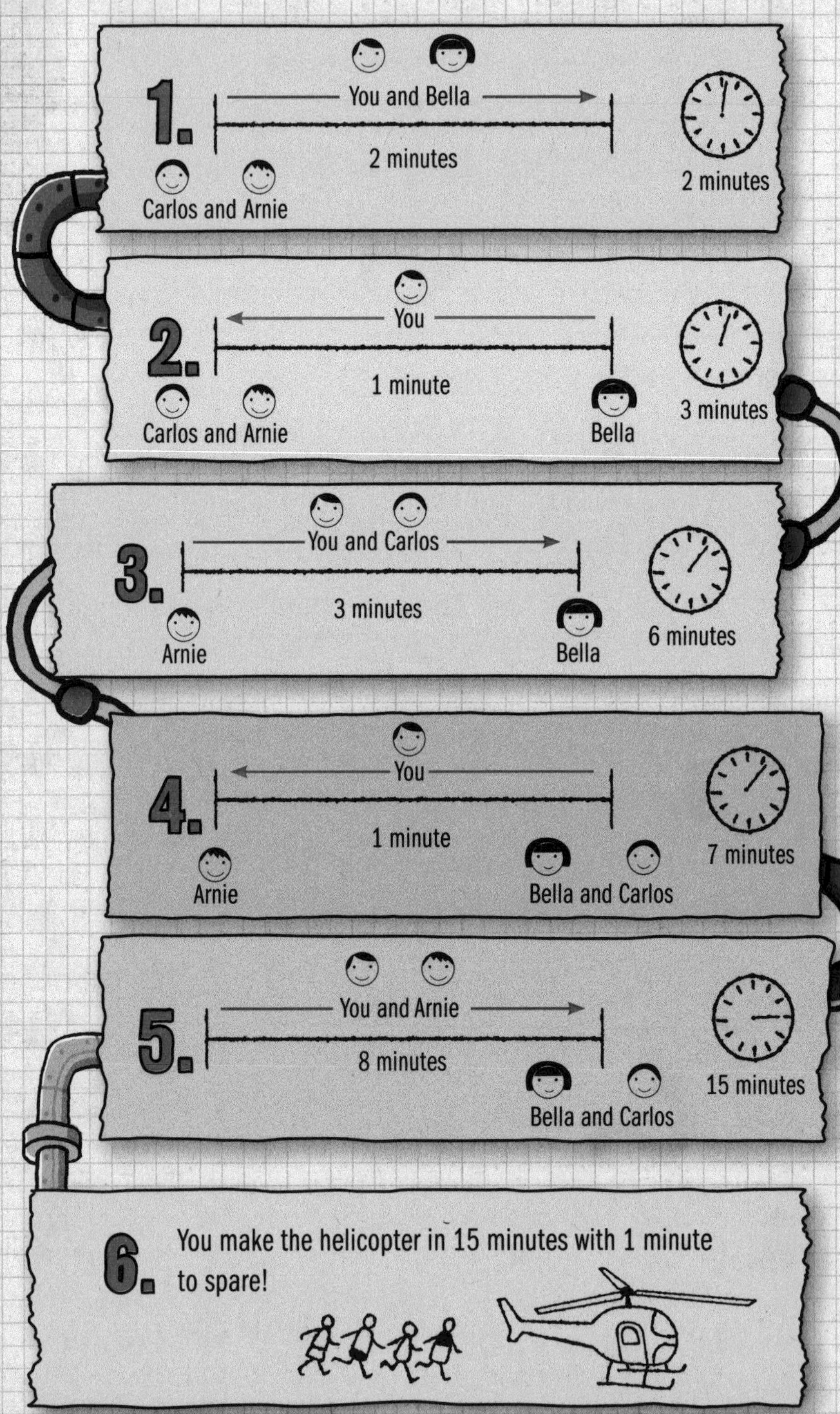

1.
You and Bella
2 minutes
Carlos and Arnie
2 minutes
2.
You
1 minute
Carlos and Arnie
Bella
3 minutes
3.
You and Carlos
3 minutes
Arnie
Bella
6 minutes
4.
You
1 minute
Arnie
Bella and Carlos
7 minutes
5.
You and Arnie
8 minutes
Bella and Carlos
15 minutes
6.
You make the helicopter in 15 minutes with 1 minute to spare!

Finding the answer to this challenge relied on remembering how fast everyone was able to walk or run in a gym class activity. Time each other at school to see how long it might take each of your friends to walk across a 400-foot-long rope bridge! You'll need 100 feet of space stretching out ahead of you, so try setting up this experiment on the playground.

YOU WILL NEED

- MEASURING TAPE
- MASKING TAPE OR CHALK
- PEN OR PENCIL
- A FEW FRIENDS (TO HAVE THEIR WALKING TIMED)
- STOPWATCH OR OTHER TIMER

THE METHOD

1. First, you need to mark off a 100-foot distance along the playground surface, measuring 5-foot sections by marking each with a small strip of masking tape.

2. Label these strips of tape with a pen every 5 feet (5 feet, 10 feet, 15 feet, and so on).

3. Have the first person stand at the start. At a signal given by the timer, the first walker should start walking at their normal pace.

4. When the stopwatch hits 8 seconds, the timer should yell "Stop!"

5. Repeat steps 3 and 4 for each person in the group, recording everyone's times.

6. Now, for each person, you have a figure telling you that they walked "x feet in 8 seconds."

7. If the rope footbridge is 400 feet long, work out how long it will take each walker to cross it by setting up a simple equation: Divide 400 by x (the distance they walked). That tells you how much longer 400 feet is, compared with the distance they walked.

8. To find out how long it would take each person to walk 400 feet, multiply 8 by whatever number you got in step 7. It should be different for every person. Could you work out a system of "The Rope Bridge" crossings, based on this information?

BRAIN BENDER

GUESSWORK? NO—GAUSSWORK!

One of the best stories in math history involves a hot-tempered teacher and a boy genius. German mathematician Carl Friedrich Gauss was only seven years old for his first math class. His teacher, Mr. Büttner, liked to give really hard assignments.

Mr. Büttner told the children to find the sum of the numbers 1 to 100. He sat down, saw to a few things on his desk, and then looked up and saw the children busy scribbling away on their slates. That is, all except one. Carl was sitting quietly with his hands folded. The slates Mr. Büttner collected were crammed full of numbers and crossings-out. Again, Carl's was the exception.

His slate simply read 5,050—the correct answer!

HOW'D HE DO IT?

Like many other great thinkers, Carl could find simple solutions. He quickly realized that the sum of the first number and the last number (1 and 100) is 101. Likewise, the sum of the second number with the second-to-last number (2 and 99) is also 101. If he continued in this pattern, each pair adds up to 101:

$$\begin{array}{rrrr} 1 & 2 & 3 \ldots & 50 \\ +100 & +99 & +98 \ldots & +51 \\ \hline 101 & 101 & 101 \ldots & 101 \end{array}$$

There are 50 pairs, each adding up to 101, so the total is $50 \times 101 = 5{,}050$. Simple! (If you're a seven year-old genius.)

ZZZZZ
VOL. BASS TREBLE

14

CHANCES OF SURVIVAL: SLIM TO NONE

SURVIVAL STRATEGIES: GEOMETRY

DEATH BY: IRATE UNCLE

THE PUNK PRANK PAYBACK

THE CHALLENGE

Your band just won the local Battle of the Bands competition, scoring not only a record deal with an independent label, but some prize money, too. To celebrate, you and your bandmates have decided to take over your uncle's one-bedroom beachside apartment in Florida while he's away. As long as you pay for your own transportation and keep the place spotlessly clean (he's a total clean freak), he's fine with you staying there. Cheap vacation!

Everything's going perfectly—that is, until the day before your uncle is scheduled to arrive home. You get up to make some breakfast. Ugh! Something's stuck on your foot! Both feet! You sit back on the bed and notice that the soles of your feet are black!

"Um, guys? Hey, what's with the floor?" you ask your bandmates.

"April Fool's!" they yell. "It's joke paint that you can just vacuum up. We 'painted' every room!"

"Are you sure it's joke paint?" you ask. The paint shows no sign of coming off your feet.

One of them grabs the paint can and reads, "Hard-wearing theatrical paint. Dries in 8 hours. Do not let paint touch unwanted wood, ceramics, or clothing. Oops."

Looks like this isn't going to be a very cheap vacation, after all. Now you have to replace all of the flooring in the apartment—before your uncle gets back into town tomorrow. The only place open on a Sunday is closing in 30 minutes—and it will take you 20 minutes to get there. You need to take some quick measurements to figure out how big each room is so you can purchase the correct amount of flooring.

Here's the floor plan of the apartment with your measurements:

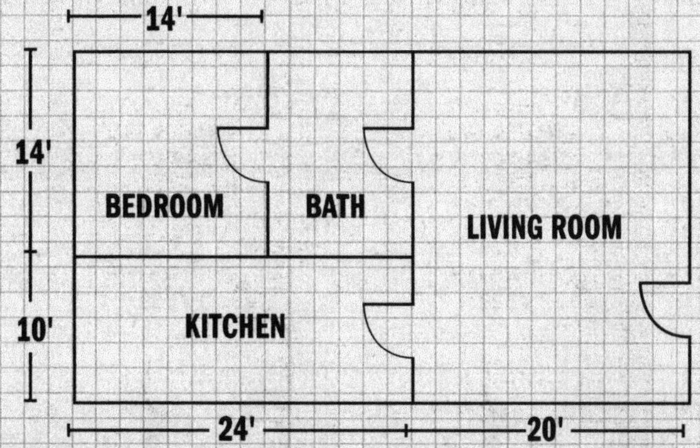

Will you be able to give the sales associate at the store exact measurements for each room with the information you have? If so, how much flooring will you need to buy for each room?

AREA OF A RECTANGLE

Finding the area of a rectangle (four sides with all right angles) is simple: Multiply the length (*l*) times width (*w*).

$$A = l \times w$$

EUCLID'S ADVICE

This problem is a good example of letting some of the "other" information you have (in this case, dimensions of other rooms) help you work out missing information.

Write down everything you know:

- **Luckily, each room has four right angles.**
- **The bedroom is a perfect square (14 feet × 14 feet).**
- **The kitchen is a rectangle (10 feet × 24 feet).**

WORKSHEET

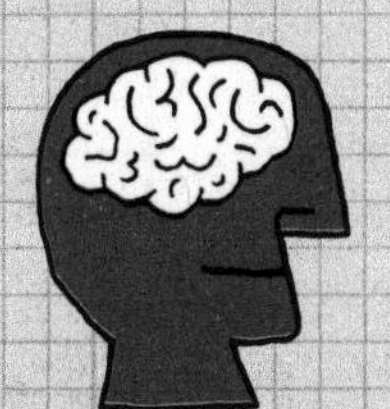
work it out.

THE SOLUTION

YES, YOU CAN GIVE EXACT MEASUREMENTS. YOU NEED TO ORDER 196 SQUARE FEET FOR THE BEDROOM, 140 SQUARE FEET FOR THE BATHROOM, 240 SQUARE FEET FOR THE KITCHEN, AND 480 SQUARE FEET FOR THE LIVING ROOM.

Solve it, step-by-step (or, in this case, room-by-room):

1. First, fill in the blanks in terms of room measurements. Since all of the rooms have right angles, parallel sides of each rectangular room will be equal to one another in length. That means you have all of the information you need to find the missing measurements:

Bedroom: 14 feet long × 14 feet wide

Bathroom: 14 feet long × 10 feet wide

Kitchen: 24 feet long × 10 feet wide

Living Room: 24 feet long × 20 feet wide

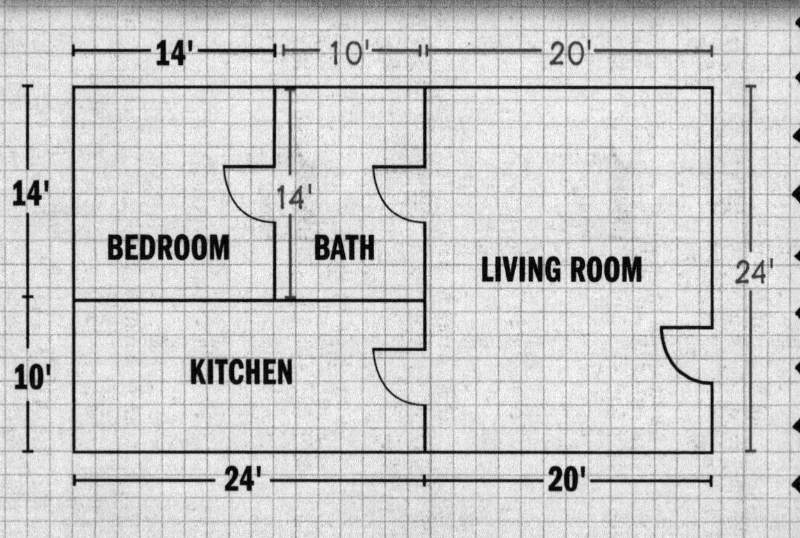

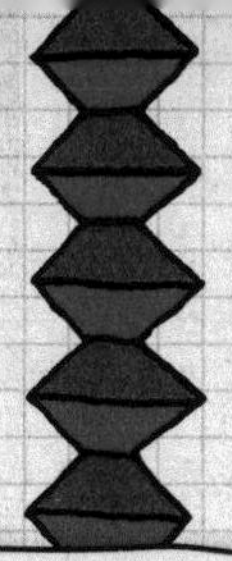

2. Now, find the area of each room, using the formula for a rectangle: **Area = length × width**

Bedroom: 14 × 14 = 196 square feet

Bathroom: 14 × 10 = 140 square feet

Kitchen: 24 × 10 = 240 square feet

Living Room: 24 × 20 = 480 square feet

Your quick measurements were enough! You can order the correct amount of flooring before your uncle returns.

MATH LAB

This activity is all about measuring and area. Instead of square feet, though, you'll be working in square inches. Just remember that the area of a rectangle is its length multiplied by its width ($A = l \times w$). And a square is a special rectangle, whose length is the same as its width.

YOU WILL NEED

- 1 SHEET OF CONSTRUCTION PAPER, CUT TO SIZE (6 INCHES BY 9 INCHES)
- RULER
- SCISSORS

THE METHOD

1. Lay the paper out on a desk or table, and get your ruler.

2. Your challenge is to use all of the paper to make 4 shapes: 2 rectangles (each with an area of 18 square inches) and 2 squares (each with an area of 9 square inches).

HINT: Use the formula for the area of a rectangle to figure out the length and width of the rectangles and squares.

3. Now it's up to you to measure and cut. Can you figure out the measurements for the shapes?

THE SOLUTION: THE 2 RECTANGLES SHOULD BE 6 INCHES BY 3 INCHES AND THE 2 SQUARES SHOULD BE 3 INCHES BY 3 INCHES.

BRAIN BENDER

THE FOUR NINES

Quick! Here's a math riddle:

Use four 9s in a math equation that equals a hundred.

Could you figure it out in 2 minutes or less?

Answer: $99 + (\frac{9}{9}) = 100$

ROUTE
66

15

CHANCES OF SURVIVAL: SLIM TO NONE

SURVIVAL STRATEGIES: RATIOS AND PROPORTIONS

DEATH BY: MOTHER NATURE

TORNADO ON YOUR TAIL!

THE CHALLENGE

You're speeding along a flat country road in western Kansas, with the season's biggest tornado appearing to follow you in the rearview mirror—and it's getting closer.

Note to self: Never, ever again agree to any request that begins, "Hey, my favorite sibling, can you do me a favor?"

SUPERCELLS

Sometimes the clouds that form into thunderclouds grow even larger and more powerful. These huge clouds can form what are known as supercells—extremely tall, dark towers of cloud. Everything about a normal thunderstorm is heightened—the amount of rain or even hailstones, the frequency of lightning, and most important, the speed of the wind. Supercells are the huge storm clouds that give birth to tornadoes.

It all started when your brother, Will, who likes to think of himself as a daring "storm chaser," asked you to drive him to McClintock township. You agreed—what a mistake. By the time you reached McClintock, it is a disaster! You turn left (west) out of town on the only clear road, and drive away as fast as you can. The radio news says the tornado is also moving westward, at 30 miles per hour, and that everyone is urged to take shelter.

You're going as fast as you can to the nearest shelter. You slow down as you search for one of the storm shelters that seem so easy to find when it's sunny. You park your car and continue searching when—flash . . . boom!—the lightning and thunder remind you of the approaching tornado. Instinctively, you start to count. It takes 50 seconds for the sound of thunder to reach you. Will, the amateur storm chaser, knows that sound travels at about 0.2 miles per second at your altitude.

How much longer do you have to find shelter from the tornado before everything gets swept away—including you and Will?

EUCLID'S ADVICE

Write down everything you know:

- **The tornado is heading for you at 30 miles per hour.**
- **It takes 50 seconds for the sound of thunder to reach you.**
- **You see the lightning almost at the instant it flashed because light travels so quickly.**
- **The sound of the thunder covers that same distance at 0.2 miles per second.**

WORKSHEET

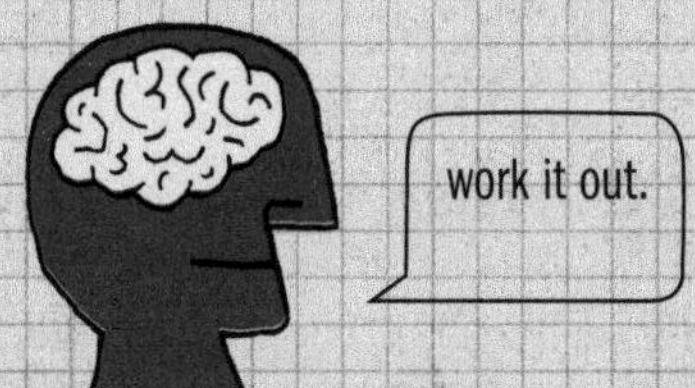

THE SOLUTION

YOU HAVE 20 MINUTES TO FIND SHELTER FROM THE TORNADO.

Solve it, step-by-step:

1. First work out how far away the tornado is. If sound travels 0.2 mile per second ($\frac{0.2}{1}$), then set up a proportional equation to figure out how many seconds it will take to travel 1 mile. Let's call this variable "s."

$$\frac{0.2}{1} = \frac{1}{s}$$

$$0.2s = 1$$

$$s = \frac{1}{0.2}$$

$$s = 5 \text{ seconds}$$

That means it will take 5 seconds for sound to travel 1 mile.

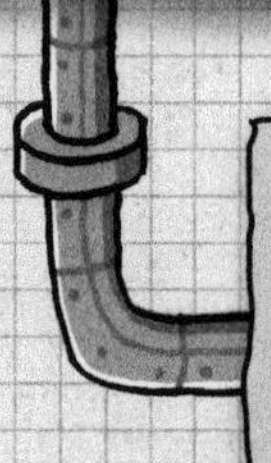

2. It took 50 seconds for the sound of thunder to reach you. If sound travels 1 mile in 5 seconds, divide 50 by 5 to find out how many miles the sound traveled (and therefore, how far away the tornado is).

$$50 \div 5 = 10 \text{ miles}$$

That means the tornado is 10 miles away from you.

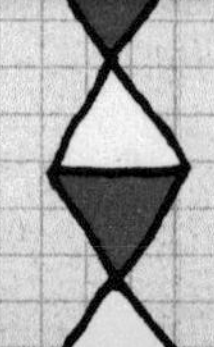

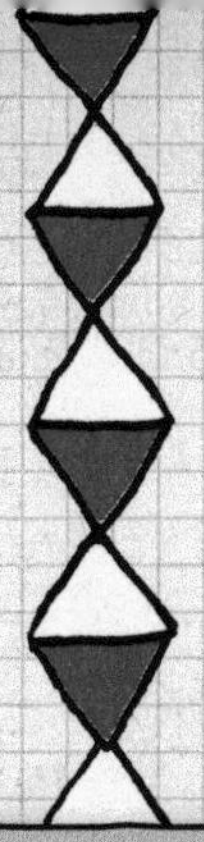

3. Next, work out how long it will take for the tornado to reach you. The tornado is traveling 30 miles per hour (60 minutes), so set up a proportional equation to figure out how many minutes it will take the tornado to travel 10 miles. Let's call this variable *t*.

$$\frac{30}{60} = \frac{0}{t}$$

$$30t = 600$$

$$t = 20 \text{ minutes}$$

That means you have 20 minutes to find shelter before the tornado reaches you.

MATH LAB

Sound travels through the air in waves at the "speed of sound." What does that really mean? Sound waves can only travel a particular distance in a particular amount of time. In "Tornado on Your Tail!" we used the figure 0.2 mile per second.

Here's a fun way to demonstrate the way waves work. While it's not exactly the same as sound waves, in this lab you'll get to understand the way waves work in water. You'll need a large—and calm—body of water to get a good result, so try to get to a pond or pool early in the day, before others arrive.

YOU WILL NEED

- CALM BODY OF WATER
- MEASURING TAPE
- 2 LONG STICKS OR SMALL STONES
- 2 FRIENDS
- STOPWATCH OR TIMER

THE METHOD

1. Decide on a spot in the pond or pool where you want to begin measuring.
2. On the shore or side of the pool, measure out a length of 20 feet and mark it with a stick or stone.

3. Have one friend stand at the 20-foot mark (on land) and a second friend as close to the "start point" (also on land) as possible. The second friend should have the timer.

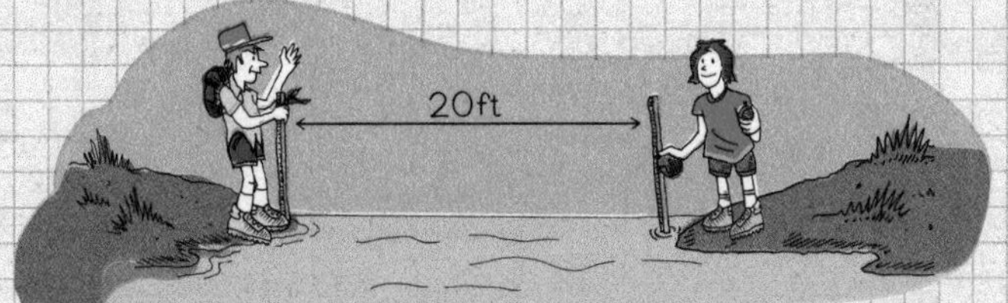

4. At a given signal, drop a stone or dip a stick into the water at the start point; your friend with the timer should start timing when it hits the water.

5. Your second friend should watch the first (outermost) ripple make its way to the 20-foot mark and shout "Stop!" when it reaches it.

6. You now have a figure telling you how long the wave took to travel 20 feet.

7. How long would it take the wave to travel 100 feet, or even 1,000 feet?

8. Finally, use your answer for 1,000 feet to estimate how long it would take for the same wave to travel 1 mile. (There are 5,280 feet in 1 mile.) Is it faster or slower than the speed of sound?

THE SOLUTION: TO FIGURE OUT HOW LONG IT TOOK THE WAVE TO TRAVEL 100 FEET, MULTIPLY THE NUMBER YOU GOT IN STEP 6 BY 5. THEN MULTIPLY THAT NUMBER BY 10 TO GET THE FIGURE FOR 1,000 FEET. FINALLY, MULTIPLY THIS LAST FIGURE BY 5 TO GET A ROUGH IDEA OF HOW LONG IT WOULD TAKE THE WAVE TO TRAVEL 1 MILE.

< PLANETARY DEFENSE >
01234
56789
500
B
R
π
6P
W
D 8000.00
C = π D
25,120 MILES
HAL9001
A 05 / 11 / B 09 22 / C 01 04 :00:00:02
ED

16

CHANCES OF SURVIVAL: SLIM TO NONE

SURVIVAL STRATEGIES: GEOMETRY

DEATH BY: ASTEROID

THE LONG WAY AROUND

THE CHALLENGE

It's the year 2133, and you're the chief engineer of EarthDefense, the intergalactic organization that protects planets in our galaxy from all manner of threats. So far you've vaporized 17 satellites that were falling out of orbit and rescued a broken-down spacecraft on its way back to Earth from the Mars colony.

Now you're facing a bigger threat. You were on the planet Pydee in a neighboring planetary system, overseeing the installation of a solar wind shield, when EarthDefense discovered a large, planet-destroying asteroid heading straight for Pydee. Luckily, your organization has an answer—a fiber-optic cable that can be wrapped around Pydee like a belt. When the asteroid gets close enough to the surface of Pydee, an electromagnetic charge can be sent through the cable, breaking up the asteroid into tiny pieces.

You were the one in charge of having the belt built. To do that, you got the accurate geological measurement of Pydee's diameter: 8,000 miles exactly. Then, you knew how to work out the distance around the planet (its circumference) by using the famous equation:

The circumference of a circle is equal to its diameter times the constant "π" (which is the Greek letter *pi*).

Or:

$C = \pi D$, where C represents the circumference and D represents the diameter of a circle.

Pi (π) is a special constant that represents certain relationships within every circle. Its decimal form, 3.141592653589..., goes on and on without end. Since writing out all those decimal places would take a long time, we often use a shortened form of π. You used 3.14, which will save on calculations, but the results will be approximate.

You plugged in the known numbers (D and π) and got:

$$C = 3.14 \times 8{,}000 = 25{,}120$$

And that's how many miles of fiber-optic cable your team produced. You explain your process to your boss, who says, "You've measured along the surface of Pydee, haven't you?"

"Um, yes," you reply.

"Well, if it's touching Pydee, the charge will be absorbed inward. We need a gap of 6 inches between Pydee and the cable. You'd better build a patch in the cable, but hurry. That asteroid is close."

You walk from the room thinking, "A patch? For something that's going all the way around a planet?!"

How long do you need to make the patch in feet, if you round to the nearest hundredth place? Is there a way to figure it out with a linear equation so you can avoid doing math with many digits?

LINEAR EQUATIONS

A linear equation is made up of two equal sets of mathematical expressions. One or more of the values, however, are unknown. These unknown values are called variables and are represented by letters, like *x* or *y*. Why are linear equations so helpful? They simplify things! You can do the same amount of math in fewer steps. And when you start solving equations with more than two variables, you'll be glad to know how to construct linear equations.

EUCLID'S ADVICE

Stay cool, and write down everything you know:

- **Pydee's diameter is 8,000 miles.**
- **There are 5,280 feet in a mile.**
- **The present cable is 25,120 miles long.**
- **But the cable really needs to be 6 inches above the surface of Pydee, which means adding 1 foot (6 inches on either side of the circle) to the diameter figure.**
- **You need to find out how much greater the circumference will be once you've accounted for that extra 1 foot: The patch will be the same as that extra amount.**

HINT: A linear equation will really help you. If you want to do all the calculations in this problem, use feet and take out your calculator!

WORKSHEET

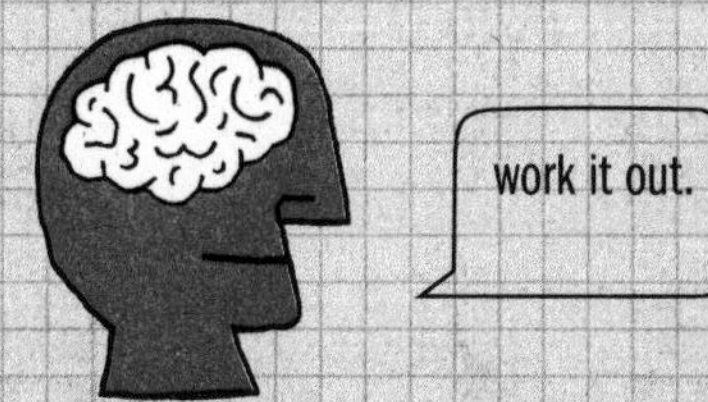
work it out.

THE SOLUTION

YOU NEED TO PRODUCE ONLY π (3.14) EXTRA FEET OF CABLE!

Solve it, step-by-step:

1. The patch will add an extra 1 foot (6 inches on each side) to the diameter of the planet Pydee. But all the measurements have been in miles, because the cable is so long.

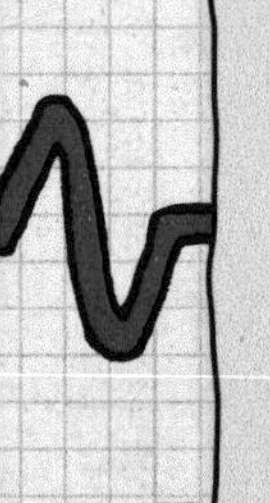

2. You can represent 8,000 miles in terms of feet (since that is the unit in which the answer is requested), and then add 1 more foot to the diameter, and multiply the new total by π (3.14) to get the new circumference.

3. But that's a lot of work. Let's try to cut down on all that calculating by creating a linear equation instead, and we will discover that the big number, *A*, doesn't actually matter in the answer. Assign the original diameter a variable (call it *A*), and assign a second variable to the extra diameter (call it *e*). In terms of *A*, the original circumference is πA.

4. Now, let's write the equation for the new circumference. Both pieces of the diameter, *A* and *e*, are added together to make the new diameter and then the sum is multiplied by π to get the new circumference.

$$\pi (A + e) = \text{new circumference}$$

5. Now use the distributive property of multiplication to write the equation like this:

$$\pi A + \pi e = \text{new circumference}$$

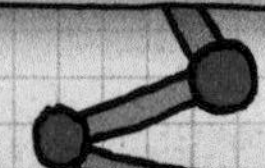

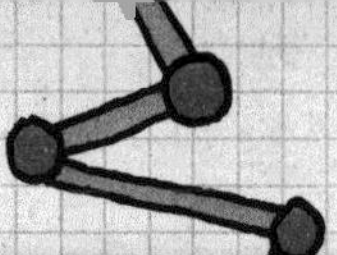

6. Since you already know the original circumference is πA, you can subtract that from the equation to get the length of cable you must splice in:

$$\text{splice length} = \text{new circumference} - \text{old circumference} = (\pi A + \pi e) - \pi A = \pi e$$

That means that the exact value of *A* doesn't matter. We say it "drops out from the equation." All you really need to do is solve for the value of πe. And what does *e* stand for? The extra 1 foot of diameter. So the splice length is:

$$\pi e = 3.14 \times 1 = 3.14 \text{ feet}$$

Whoa! That means the patch needs to be only 3.14 feet long to lift the whole cable 6 inches above the entire surface of Pydee!

7. Want to do all of the calculations to prove this? Take out your calculator and plug in these numbers. But you'll need a calculator that shows eleven digits if you want to get the correct answer. Paper and pencil might be more accurate.

First, let's find the original diameter in feet. There are 5,280 feet in 1 mile, so 8,000 miles is 8,000 x 5,280 feet, which is 42,240,000 feet. After you add 6 inches to each side of Pydee's diameter, the new diameter is 42,240,001 feet. We multiply each of these large numbers by π to find the old and new circumferences:

$$42{,}240{,}000 \times 3.14 = 132{,}633{,}600$$

$$42{,}240{,}001 \times 3.14 = 132{,}633{,}603.14$$

Okay, now subtract the original circumference from the new circumference:

$$132{,}633{,}603.14 - 132{,}633{,}600 = 3.14$$

That's π feet! Amazing!

MATH LAB

That challenge is one to make you shake your head and wonder whether you really got it right. But it is the right answer, and you can re-create that sense of wonder by doing some calculations of your own. You won't have to travel around a planet, and you won't need to work in miles, or even feet: Stick to inches and you'll still be amazed.

Remember that the diameter (D) of a circle is a line that passes all the way through the center of a circle and the radius (r) is halfway across. The formula for the circumference (C) of a circle is either:

$$C = \pi D \text{ or: } C = 2\pi r$$

YOU WILL NEED

- 2 SHEETS OF BLANK PAPER
- COMPASS (FOR MATH, NOT FOR HIKING!)
- STRING (AT LEAST 36 INCHES LONG)
- RULER
- PENCIL

THE METHOD

1. Set the point of the compass in the center of a sheet of paper and measure exactly 1 inch out (that sets the radius of the circle to 1 inch).

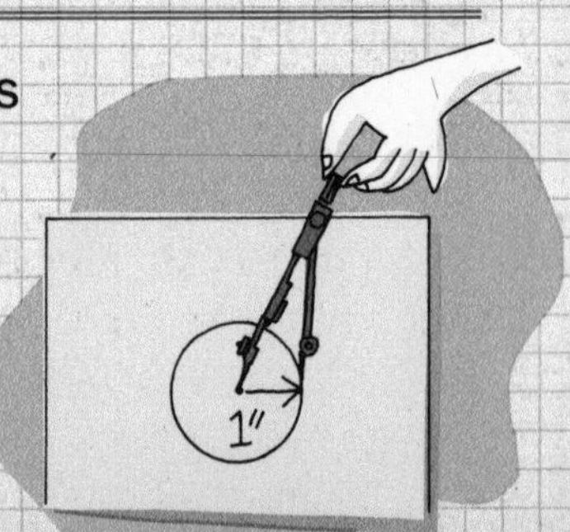

2. Now draw a circle carefully, using that setting of the compass.

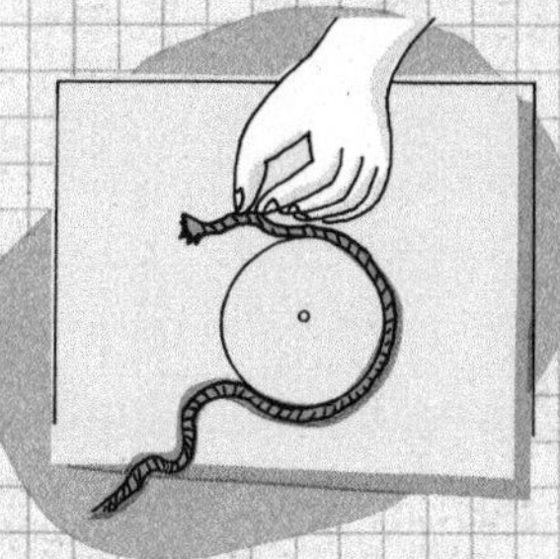

3. Take the string and carefully measure around the circle itself (you're measuring the circumference when you do that). Mark the string with a dot.

4. Measure the string with the ruler from the end to the dot. On a separate sheet of paper, write that figure down, next to a note that says: "Diameter: 2 inches, radius: 1 inch."

5. Now lengthen the compass by $\frac{1}{2}$ inch, so that it is set at $1\frac{1}{2}$ inches.

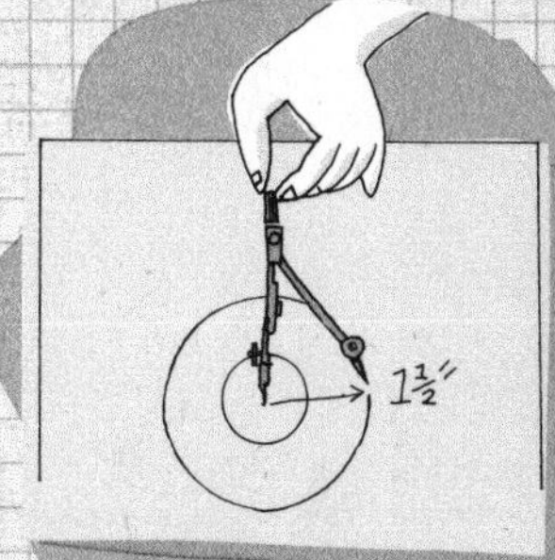

6. Draw a circle with this radius using the same center as the first circle.

7. Repeat steps 3 and 4, drawing a new circle with a radius $\frac{1}{2}$ inch longer and recording the new radius and diameter.

8. Continue like this, increasing the radius by $\frac{1}{2}$ inch each time.

9. Do you notice a pattern in the size of the circles and the way the radius and diameter increased?

THE SOLUTION: BY INCREASING THE RADIUS BY $\frac{1}{2}$ INCH (AND THE DIAMETER BY 1 INCH), THE CIRCUMFERENCE IS ONLY INCREASING BY 3.14 (π) EACH TIME. MAKES SENSE WHEN YOU LOOK AT THE EQUATION FOR THE CIRCUMFERENCE OF A CIRCLE AGAIN, DOESN'T IT?

PRESS
and
WAIT

17

CHANCES OF SURVIVAL: SLIM TO NONE

SURVIVAL STRATEGIES: ANALYTICAL THINKING

DEATH BY: CRAZY NEIGHBOR

THE CHALLENGE

Life seemed so much simpler when the only "evil masterminds" were the ones you saw in those James Bond movies that your dad likes to watch. Who would have thought that you'd be held captive by one right now, when you'd normally be getting ready for soccer practice?

KEELHAULING

Danger ahead! This gruesome punishment was the one sailors feared most in the 17th and 18th centuries. A sailor would be tied to a rope that looped under the ship's keel (the deepest point under the ship) and thrown overboard. Then he would be pulled by the rope either the width or the length of the ship. Many sailors drowned while being keelhauled; others had their skin torn to shreds by the sharp barnacles that were stuck to the bottom of the ship.

"You like my little house, do you?" asks the old man. "Take a look at the marvels I have here. Shrunken heads from the South Pacific. A wolf skull from the Badlands of North Dakota. And sand-filled hourglasses from a sunken pirate ship in the Caribbean—Redbeard's. One hourglass is timed for 9 minutes and the other for 13 minutes: The first was how long it took to give a man 100 lashes and the other was how long Redbeard would keelhaul those who displeased him.

"You will learn your punishment tomorrow," he continues. "And don't think you can escape through this door. To open it, you have to press this button and then wait exactly 30 minutes before pressing it again. Try it too soon or leave it just 30 seconds too long, and it stays shut. Oh—I'll take your watch and phone, please," he says, slamming the door behind him.

How can you use the hourglasses in a series of steps to help you measure 30 minutes and time your escape?

EUCLID'S ADVICE

Write down everything you know:

- **The only real chance is to use the door, with its strange lock timer.**
- **You need to find some way to gauge 30 minutes accurately.**
- **The only timing devices are the 2 pirate-ship hourglasses: One measures exactly 9 minutes and the other measures exactly 13 minutes.**

HINT: Draw a line chart to help you with each step.

WORKSHEET

THE SOLUTION

YOU CAN USE THE HOURGLASSES IN COMBINATION TO WORK OUT 30 MINUTES ACCURATELY.

There is more than one solution to this problem. Here's one way to solve it, step-by-step:

1. Set the 2 hourglasses up so that they are both empty on the top and full on the bottom.

2. Flip both hourglasses over to start the 30-minute timing. Press the button on the door. Let's draw a line chart to keep track of each step.

3. When the small one empties, flip the small one over.

9 minutes have gone by.

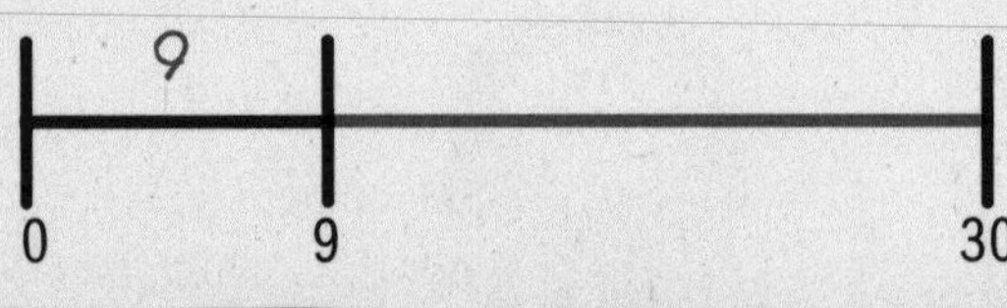

9 min.

4. When the large one empties, do nothing to it but flip the small one again.

13 minutes have gone by.

NOTE: You've flipped the small one before it could fully empty. You have reset the small timer for the same 4 minutes' of sand that you just timed.

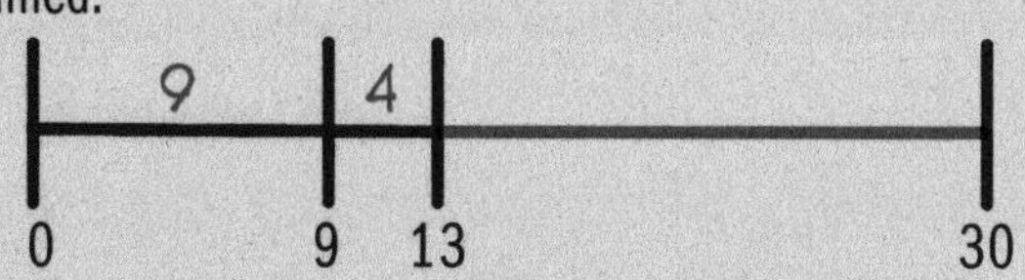

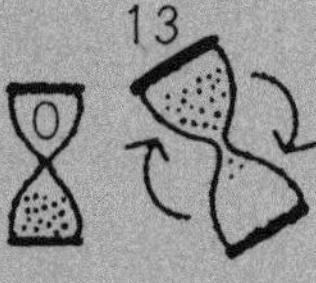

5. When the small one empties, do nothing to it but flip the large one again.

17 minutes have gone by.

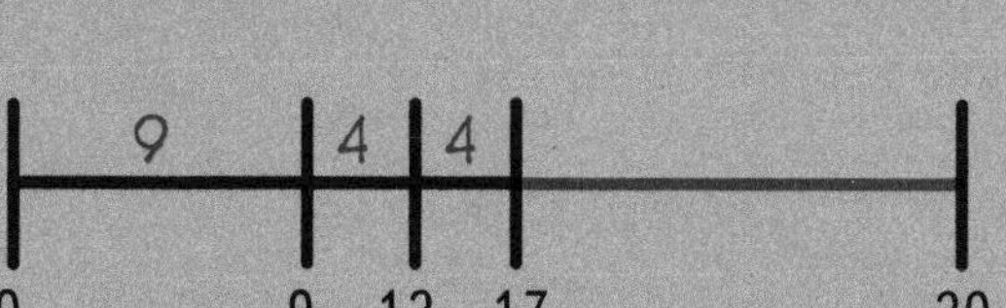

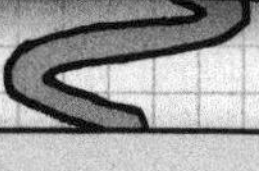

6. This large hourglass takes 13 minutes to empty.

30 minutes have gone by.

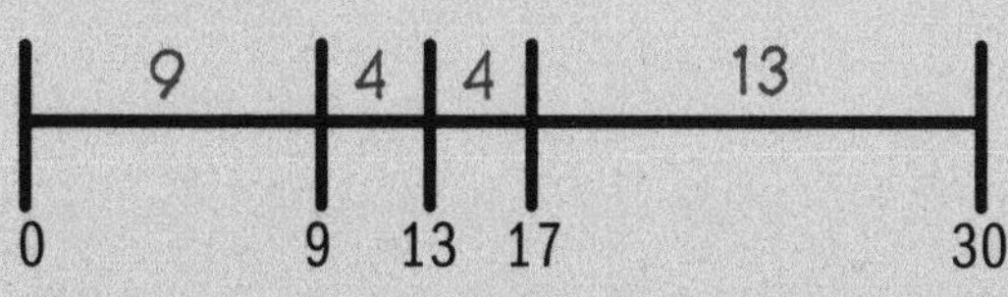

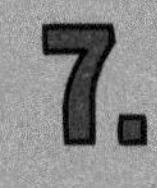

7. Press the button on the door again to open it. You're free!

MATH LAB

You could really get a feel for this challenge by doing it with an hourglass you have built yourself. You might not find yourself measuring things by the hour, but you will have built a consistent timepiece. Of course, you'd need to make 2 of them—with different amounts of sand—to really match the challenge—but to get the hang of it, just make one first.

YOU WILL NEED

- AN ADULT TO HELP YOU WITH THE SHARP PARTS
- 2 SMALL IDENTICAL PLASTIC DRINK BOTTLES, CLEANED AND DRIED (THE SMALLER THE BETTER)
- FUNNEL
- SMALL AMOUNT OF SAND (ENOUGH TO FILL ONE OF THE BOTTLES HALFWAY)
- SHARP KNIFE OR NAIL
- 1 PLASTIC CAP FROM ONE OF THE BOTTLES
- DUCT TAPE
- CLOCK OR STOPWATCH

THE METHOD

1. Use the funnel to help you fill one bottle halfway with sand.

2. Ask an adult to help you poke a small hole in the plastic cap, using the knife or nail.

3. Screw the cap onto the bottle that has sand in it.

4. Place the empty bottle upside down over the bottle with sand and align the bottle mouths so that they are straight.

5. Carefully tape the bottle mouths together, making sure the mouth of the empty bottle is aligned with the cap of the other bottle.

6. Make sure that the bottles are securely taped together.

7. Check the time on a clock, and flip the hourglass over. You may need to hold the base of the hourglass at first to keep it steady.

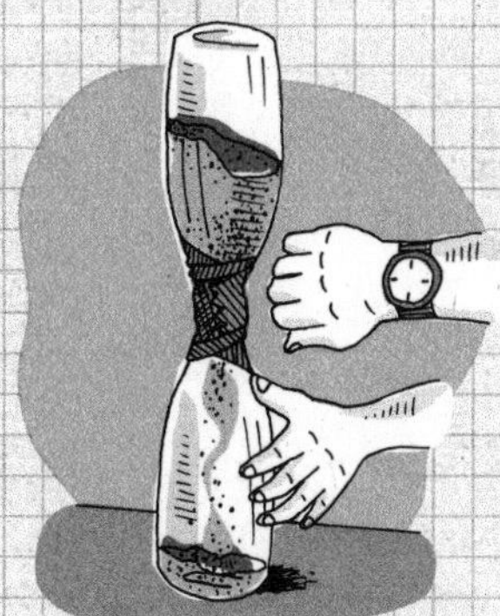

8. Check the time again when the top bottle is emptied of sand. That is now the time this hourglass measures.

9. You can add sand to make it run longer or remove sand to make the time shorter.

120
SECONDS

18

CHANCES OF SURVIVAL: SLIM TO NONE

SURVIVAL STRATEGIES: RATIOS AND PROPORTIONS

DEATH BY: SPACECRAFT

THE FINAL COUNTDOWN

THE CHALLENGE

NASA has selected you for a top secret, one-person mission to orbit the Earth and collect valuable data about one of our satellites. No one's given you the details, but you're pretty sure the CIA is involved, so you know this intelligence is really important. You've just completed the 14-hour mission and reentered the Earth's atmosphere, splashing down into the Atlantic Ocean, right on schedule. A nearby aircraft carrier was meant to launch a rescue helicopter to pluck you from the sea and put you safely onto the carrier deck.

Except there has been no sign of the helicopter. It's a good thing you never panic (because this is a prime panicking situation): No matter whether you're rereading your favorite book or being chased by a grizzly bear, your pulse remains a steady 72 beats per minute.

Then you realize something else—you're currently stuck in an airtight capsule. You figure there are 2 more minutes of oxygen in the capsule, so it's time to blow open the hatch yourself. Think through what you know and what you have to do.

First of all, the hatch has some built-in defense mechanisms so it can't be opened accidentally. There's a combination you have to enter, but then you have to wait exactly 35 seconds before turning the handle to open the hatch. A second too soon, or too late, and you have to start from scratch. But just over 14 hours ago, you took off your wristwatch. You kissed your only means of timing goodbye when you did that. Or did you?

Using the information you have, how can you count 35 seconds exactly?

EUCLID'S ADVICE

Write down everything you know:

- **Your heart beats at a steady 72 beats per minute, no matter what.**
- **You have 2 minutes worth of air left.**
- **You need to wait exactly 35 seconds after entering in the code before opening the capsule's hatch.**

WORKSHEET

THE SOLUTION

COUNT 42 OF YOUR HEARTBEATS AND THEN OPEN THE HATCH.

Solve it, step-by-step:

1. Since you are always calm under pressure, your heartbeats remain steady and can be used instead of a watch. Your heart beats 72 times per minute. Set up a ratio to represent this data.

$$\frac{72 \text{ beats}}{60 \text{ seconds}}$$

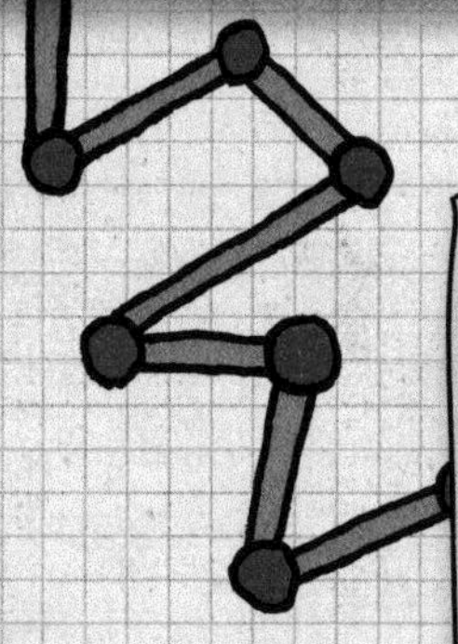

2. Now set up a ratio to represent how many times your heart beats in 35 seconds (or $\frac{1}{2}$ minute). Let's call this variable *h*.

$$\frac{h \text{ beats}}{35 \text{ seconds}}$$

3. Since you're solving for a value that is a fraction of a ratio you already know, these ratios are in proportion to one another. Set them equal to each other.

$$\frac{72 \text{ beats}}{60 \text{ seconds}} = \frac{h \text{ beats}}{35 \text{ seconds}}$$

4. Cross-multiply and solve for *h*.

$$60h = 2{,}520$$
$$h = 42$$

That means that in 35 seconds, your heart will beat 42 times.

It's a good thing you can stay calm under pressure!

You can test your own pulse easily. All you'll need is a watch or timer that counts seconds. Use the index and middle finger of one hand to feel the inside of your wrist on your other hand, just below the thumb. Gently move the fingers around until you feel a slight beating (that's your pulse).

Keep your fingers on the pulse and count the beats for exactly 30 seconds.

How can you use that data to find your pulse rate in beats per minute (bpm)?

YOU WILL NEED

- **WATCH OR TIMER**

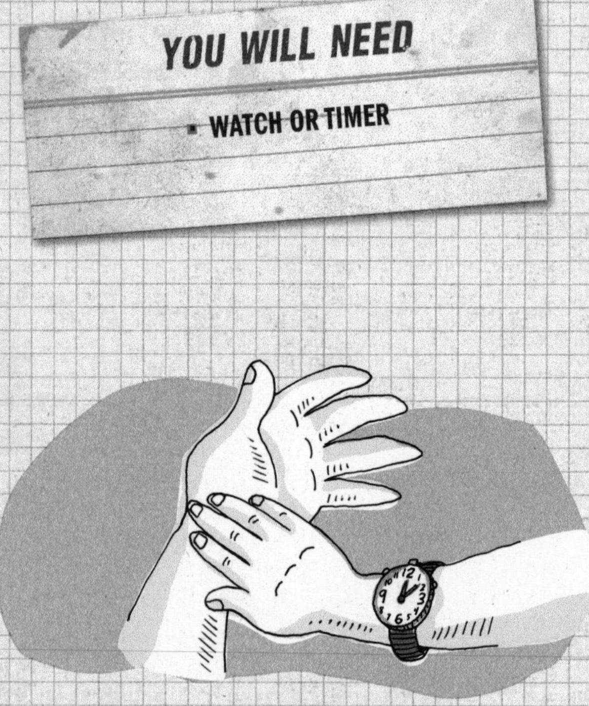

THE SOLUTION: DOUBLE THAT AMOUNT TO GET YOUR PULSE RATE IN BEATS PER MINUTE (BPM).

BRAIN BENDER

THE "1,089 TRICK"

Here's a nice trick you can play on a friend. Just make sure he has a pencil and paper because he's going to need to do some calculations. And the best way for you to perform this trick is either blindfolded or with your back to your friend.

It works most smoothly if you call out, "Step 1," "Step 2," and so on, and say the steps to your friend word for word. Practice this routine so you have it memorized:

Step 1: Think of a 3-digit number, with decreasing digits (from left to right) and write it down.

Step 2: Reverse the number you have just written down, so that this number has increasing digits.

Step 3: Subtract the number in step 2 from the original number (step 1).

Step 4: Now reverse the number you got in step 3.

Step 5: Add the numbers from steps 3 and 4.

At this point, you should interrupt and give them the answer: 1,089!

It always works, provided you start with a 3-digit number with decreasing digits.

STORE
24 HOUR
CAB

19

CHANCES OF SURVIVAL: YOU'RE DEAD

SURVIVAL STRATEGIES: EXPRESSIONS AND EQUATIONS

DEATH BY: BLOOD LOSS

THE CHALLENGE

You never believed in vampires—until you saw one for yourself. He's new in town, a strange-looking dude, who up until now seems to have been living off of the stray cats in the neighborhood. Problem is, no one else has ever seen him but you. And no one believes you—no one except your best friend, Jamie, who happens to be an expert on vampires. According to Jamie, vampires only come out at night, and they only feed two times a month. Feeding means sucking the blood of a human, and after they're through, that person becomes a vampire, too. One month later, these new vampires will each be capable of turning 2 more people into vampires.

"But how come he only feeds on cats?" you ask Jamie.

"They're just an appetizer," Jamie explains. "At the next full moon, he'll be looking for human blood. The good news is that there's only one vampire in town. How much harm could a single vampire do?"

"A lot!" you answer. "There are 500,000 people living in this town, right? That means, unless we find the vampire before the next full moon, our town will soon be completely taken over by vampires!" Jamie doesn't believe you, so you have to prove it to him.

If the vampires feed only on people in your town, approximately how many months will it take for your 500,000-person town to become populated entirely by vampires?

EUCLID'S ADVICE

Remember the power of 3! Things can get out of control pretty quickly when numbers continue to triple. Once you figure out the pattern in which the vampires are increasing, creating an algebraic linear equation may be helpful. You'll need to assign two variables, one to represent the current number of vampires (a value you know), and another to represent the new number of vampires (the value you're solving for). Then, set up a table, or chart, to organize your data.

But first, write down everything you know:

- **There is currently only 1 vampire in town.**
- **There are 500,000 people who live in town.**
- **Every month, 1 vampire feeds on 2 humans, turning both of them into vampires.**

WORKSHEET

THE SOLUTION

IN 12 MONTHS, THE ENTIRE TOWN WILL BE MADE UP OF VAMPIRES.

Solve it, step-by-step:

1. First, let's find the pattern. Consider that the vampire population trples each month because each vampire feeds on 2 humans, turning each of them into a vampire.

2. At the end of 1 month, 2 humans will have become vampires.

$$1 \times 2 = 2 \text{ vampires}$$

Add these 2 to the original vampire and it puts the total vampire population at 3.

$$2 + 1 = 3 \text{ vampires}$$

3. In the following month, each of these 3 vampires will then transform 2 more humans into vampires, making 6 new vampires.

$$3 \times 2 = 6 \text{ vampires}$$

Add these 6 to the original 3, and the total vampire population would be 9.

$$6 + 3 = 9 \text{ vampires}$$

4. These 9 each turn 2 more humans into vampires by the end of the third month, making the vampire population 27.

$$(9 \times 2) + 9 = 27 \text{ vampires}$$

5. Do you see a pattern emerging? To find the total number of vampires each month, multiply the current number of vampires by 2 and then add the current number of vampires to that number. This will give you the new total number of vampires in that month. Written as an equation, it would look like this:

$$v = \text{the current number of vampires}$$
$$x = \text{the total number of vampires}$$
$$(v \times 2) + v = x$$

6. To solve for the total number of vampires (x), you multiply the current number of vampires (v) by 2, and then add v to get x.

Continue the pattern until you figure out how many months it will take to create at least as many vampires as there are townspeople (500,000).

Month	"Current" Vampires	"New" Vampires	Total Vampires
0	1	0	1
1	1	2	3
2	3	6	9
3	9	18	27
4	27	54	81
5	81	162	243
6	243	486	729
7	729	1,458	2,187
8	2,187	4,374	6,561
9	6,561	13,122	19,683
10	19,683	39,366	59,049
11	59,049	118,098	177,147
12	177,147	354,294	531,441

If you continue in this fashion, the numbers really start to climb. Now you can show Jamie why it's important you get this vampire *before* the next full moon!

A story from India relates how chess was invented by the Sissa ibn Dahir, a wise man who taught King Shihram how to play the game. The ruler was delighted and asked the sissa to decide on what he wanted as a prize.

"I am a simple man, and ask only for a simple reward of rice," the sissa said. "Lay your chessboard there and place a single grain of rice on the first square. Place 2 grains (double the amount) on the second square and 4 grains (double the previous amount) on the next square, and so on through all the squares. Remember—this is a simple request."

That's all he asked. King Shihram agreed, and asked for a servant to lay out the chessboard and to fetch some rice. And since the reward is so simple, it's the next lab in this book. Is it also the simplest activity in these pages, or the hardest? You decide.

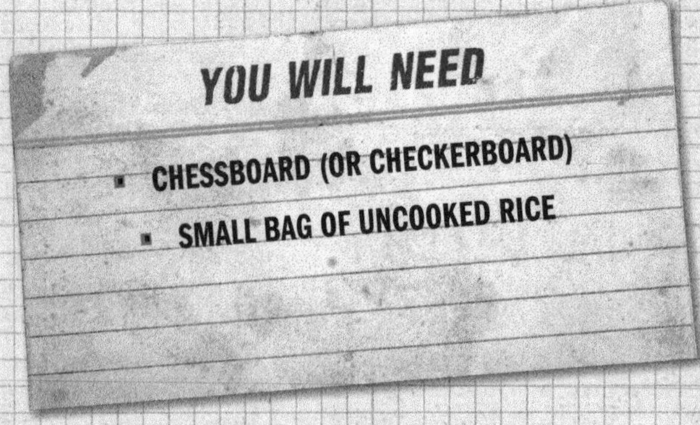

THE METHOD

1. Follow the sissa's instructions and place 1 grain of rice on the first square, 2 on the second, 4 on the third, and 8 on the fourth.

2. Now stop for a minute and do some calculations: You need to put 128 grains on the eighth square, which is at the end of the first row. But there are 7 more rows, and the number keeps doubling! By the end of the second row, you'd have reached about 32,000 grains, and just at the start of the third row, it would be double *that*. Yikes!

The sissa's request creates a sequence that mathematicians and scientists call *exponential,* which rises much, much faster than a sequence in which you add the same amount each time to move from one step to the next. That sort of a sequence is called *linear*.

You probably gave up by about the end of the first row, but if you did go all the way to the end, you'd finish up with this many rice grains on the last (sixty-fourth) square:

18,446,744,073,709,551,615

which in other words is: 18 pentillion, 446 quadrillion, 744 trillion, 73 billion, 709 million, 551 thousand, 615.

That's a lot of rice!

BRAIN BENDER

TWO MINUTES

The following statistics have been gathered from a wide range of sources. They all represent what happens in 2 minutes. But we've jumbled up the numbers in the right column and you've got to rearrange them to correctly match the events in the left column. Are you up for it? You have . . . 2 minutes!

1. Water urinated by all humans (gallons)	a. 27
2. Tons of garbage produced	b. 15,122
3. World deaths	c. 308
4. Lightning strikes	d. 3,577,938
5. Meteorites entering atmosphere	e. 158,728
6. World tobacco deaths	f. 19
7. Wall posts on Facebook	g. 11,911
8. World births	h. 160,404,800,000
9. Trees cut down	i. 209
10. Pints of blood pumped	j. 17

Answers:
1=d, 2=j, 3=i, 4=g, 5=a, 6=f, 7=e, 8=c, 9=b, 10=h

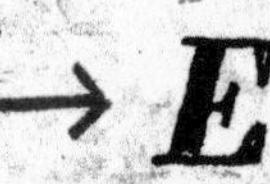

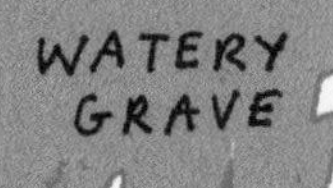

SEA SERPENT
ICEBERGS
STORMY SEAS
SHARK-INFESTED WATERS
N
MAN OVERBOARD
CERTAIN DEATH
W
E
S
IMPENDING DOOM
WATERY GRAVE
JAGGED ROCKS
CANNIBAL ISLAND
SHIPWRECK
DAVY JONE'S LOCKER
GIANT SQUID
PIRATES

20 | **CHANCES OF SURVIVAL:** YOU'RE DEAD

SURVIVAL STRATEGIES: EXPRESSIONS AND EQUATIONS; UNIT RATE

DEATH BY: MUTINY

THE CHALLENGE

You are the captain of a galleon setting off for the New World. By now you've accepted the common theory that the Earth is round. If you set sail in one direction, eventually you'll return to where you started. You've been at sea for nine weeks, and for the last few days, your progress across the Atlantic Ocean has been slow but steady.

ASTROLABES

An astrolabe was a device first invented in Greece 2,200 years ago, and became one of the earliest known navigational instruments for mariners. Astrolabes are complicated handheld instruments that help viewers locate and predict the movements of the Moon, planets, and stars. The mariner's astrolabe, developed about 500 years ago, was a simpler instrument to measure the height of the Sun (or of Polaris) above the horizon. Knowing that figure, sailors could figure out on what latitude they were located and whether they were heading toward Canada or Mexico.

Recently, you have begun to notice unrest among your crew. Then, on your 63rd day at sea, they gather silently in front of you on the deck. The first mate looks menacing, with his teeth clenched on a long-bladed knife. There's only one word to describe what is happening—mutiny.

The first mate stops just two paces in front of you. He takes the knife out of his mouth, wipes it carefully on his shirt, and speaks: "Well, captain, we've been at sea nine long weeks and there's still no sign of land. We've taken your word for a lot of things—that the Earth is round, that we'd reach

KNOTS

Sailors use different measurements for distance and speed through the water than we do on land. A nautical mile represents distance, and a knot represents speed. One knot is one nautical mile per hour. Why call it a knot? It comes from the way sailors used to measure their speed. Sailors would use a wedge-shaped piece of wood attached to a line with a knot tied in it every 47 feet, 3 inches—this was the distance that a ship would have to travel every 30 seconds if it were sailing at one knot. They would then throw the piece of wood overboard and count the number of knots that were pulled off the ship over a 30-second period of time (which they measured with an hourglass). That number of knots was then considered the ship's speed in knots (or nautical miles per hour).

land if we kept sailing west, and that the New World would be full of gold and jewels. So far we have no proof of any of this . . . and we're running out of fresh water and food."

He looks around at the crew for approval. "You say we've traveled 2,773 miles of the 3,520 miles to Cuba, and that we've stayed on course thanks to this trinket you call an astrolabe. That still leaves 747 miles in our journey. I reckon that the crew won't take more than another week of this. So, we've come up with a little demand, haven't we, lads?

"We'll time the nautical miles per hour, or knots, we are traveling. The wind is likely to remain steady for another week, so we can work from that figure whether we'll be pulling into port at Cuba by the end of the week . . . or whether you might fall overboard 'accidentally' and we take this ship to home waters."

At least how many "knots" must the ship's speed be to get you to Cuba in 7 days? Round your answer to the nearest whole number.

EUCLID'S ADVICE

Write down everything you know:

- **You've travelled 2,773 miles of the 3,520 miles to Cuba, so you have 747 miles of your journey left.**
- **One knot is the same as one nautical mile per hour (both measure speed).**
- **You have 7 days to make the rest of the journey to Cuba.**

HINT: 1 mile = 0.9 nautical mile (approximately).

WORKSHEET

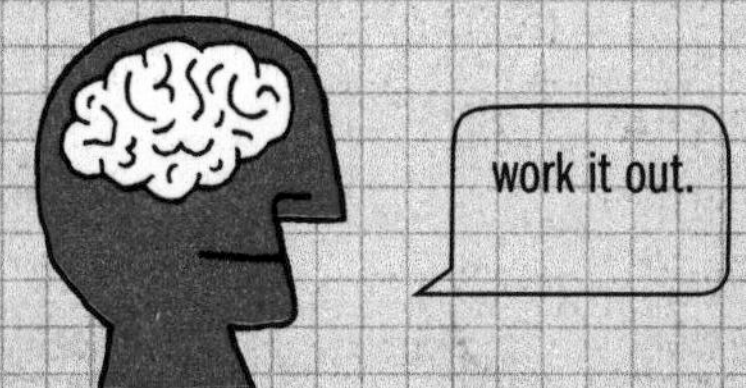
work it out.

THE SOLUTION

YOU MUST BE TRAVELING AT A SPEED OF AT LEAST 4 KNOTS, OR NAUTICAL MILES PER HOUR, TO MAKE IT TO CUBA IN 7 DAYS.

Solve it, step-by-step:

1. Since you need your answer to be in nautical miles per hour, you will need to convert the measurements you have (miles and days) to the measurements you need (nautical miles and hours).

Start by converting the distance you still need to travel (which you have in miles) to nautical miles, if 1 mile = 0.9 nautical mile.

Distance to travel to Cuba: 747 miles

Set up a proportion and cross-multiply to solve.

747 miles = 672.3 nautical miles

$$\frac{1 \text{ mile}}{0.9 \text{ nautical mile}} = \frac{747 \text{ miles}}{x \text{ nautical mile}}$$

$$x = 672.3$$

2. Next, convert the days you have left to travel until your crew throws you overboard (7) into hours. Set up a proportion and cross-multiply to solve.

$$\frac{24 \text{ hours}}{1 \text{ day}} = \frac{x \text{ hours}}{7 \text{ days}}$$

$$168 = x$$

That means there are 168 hours in 7 days.

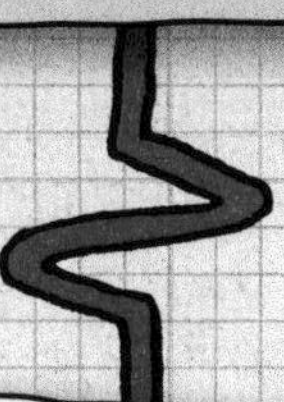

3. Now that you've converted all of the measurements into the proper units, you can set up another proportion to solve for the minimum speed in nautical miles per hour (or knots) at which you'll need to travel 672.3 nautical miles in 168 hours.

$$\frac{672.3}{168} = \frac{x}{1}$$

$$168x = 672.3$$

$x = 4.002$ (approximately)

Rounded to the nearest whole number, $x = 4$ nautical miles per hour (or knots).

That means you'll need to travel at a speed of at least 4 knots in order to make it to Cuba in 7 days.

You can make your own version of a mariner's astrolabe with some pretty basic objects. Look through it to find the angle of the Moon, but remember that you should never, ever use it to look directly at the Sun.

YOU WILL NEED

- STRING
- RULER
- SCISSORS
- PLASTIC PROTRACTOR (WITH SMALL HOLE HALFWAY ALONG THE FLAT EDGE)
- SMALL WEIGHT (LIKE A WASHER)
- TAPE
- DRINKING STRAW
- PENCIL
- ONE 4-BY-4-INCH PIECE OF CARDBOARD OR CONSTRUCTION PAPER
- FRIEND, WITH PAPER AND PENCIL

THE METHOD

1. Cut a 10-inch length of string and tie a knot at one end.

2. Feed the other end of the string through the hole in the protractor until the knot catches. (Tie another layer of knot if the string passes through.)

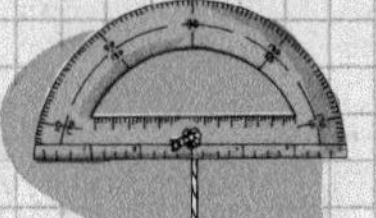

3. Tie or tape the weight to the other end of the string.

4. Tape the straw along the flat edge of the protractor so that one end extends several inches beyond it.

5. With the pencil, poke a hole in the center of the construction paper, just big enough for the straw to pass through snugly.

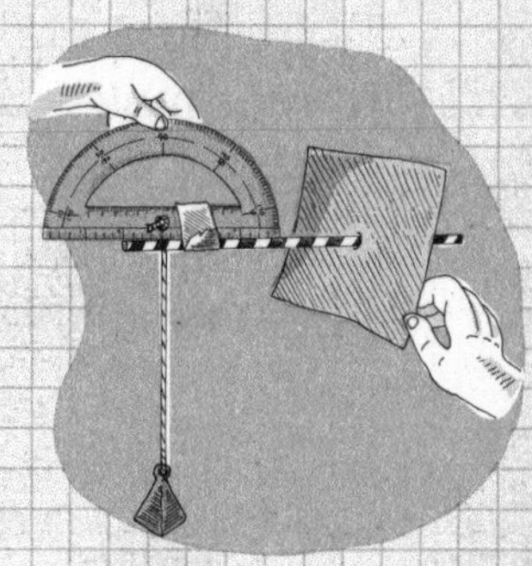

6. Slide the construction paper along the straw so that it touches the edge of the protractor.

USING YOUR MARINER'S ASTROLABE

- Hold the astrolabe so that the curved side points to the ground and the weight hangs freely.
- Look through the end of the straw that juts out, and aim it at an object (such as the Moon, the top of a building, or a distant tree).
- Hold it steady while your friend records where the string passes the measurements on the protractor. Your friend should read the scale that runs from 0 to 90.
- Now subtract the number you noted on the protractor from 90. That number is the altitude (in degrees above the horizon) of the target object.

WARNING! Never (ever!) look directly at the Sun.

110 FT
120 FT

21

CHANCES OF SURVIVAL: YOU'RE DEAD

SURVIVAL STRATEGIES: EXPRESSIONS AND EQUATIONS

DEATH BY: SCUBA MALFUNCTION

THE CHALLENGE

You are a treasure hunter. After spending years studying old charts and diaries to find where Redbeard's pirate ship sank in 1712—with its cargo of silver and jewels and his famous diamond-encrusted sword—you're finally close. The treasure you seek is 120 feet beneath you in the clear water of the Caribbean Sea. Now it's time to dive.

WHAT ARE THE BENDS, ANYWAY?

Water pressure increases the deeper you go. That increased pressure causes some of the nitrogen gas (which you breathe in normally) to go into solution, just like carbon dioxide goes into solution in a can of soda. Coming back up to the surface of the ocean is like opening the can of soda. If you do it too fast, the nitrogen "bubbles up" inside your body, possibly causing a lot of harm. It's like opening a can of soda that you've shaken and having it foam out. "Decompression stops" along the way up prevent decompression sickness, or "the bends," by allowing the nitrogen to escape safely. This is like when you open a can of soda slowly to allow the gas to escape calmly.

You drop a marker line that is marked in 5-foot intervals, so when you're down in the water, you know exactly how far you are from the surface.

It doesn't take long to get to the bottom—just 5 minutes. And then you see it: the treasure chest! But where is the sword? Before you start looking for it, you want to know exactly how much time you can spend down there before having to head back up. Your scuba tank gives you 1 hour's worth of air, and you'll want to avoid getting "the bends" on the way up by making decompression stops at specific depths to help your body adjust to the change in pressure. Luckily, your trusty wrist computer will tell you exactly how long you can spend underwater, taking into account where and when to make those stops, but . . . oh no! It's not on your wrist! You realize you left it back onboard your ship—the ship that is now 120 feet above you—and put on your regular (waterproof) watch instead.

Okay, don't panic. Think. Remember all you can from your years of scuba training:

1. The first 2-minute decompression stop should be taken at $\frac{1}{2}$ your maximum depth.

2. After you begin decompression stops, you shouldn't go up faster than 1 minute per every 10 feet.

3. Also, you have to wait 1 minute between these 10-foot ascents.

4. You always have to stop for 5 minutes at the final 15-foot marker. After that, you can go up without any more stops.

5. Scuba divers are cautious: They always round numbers up (meaning, in this case, a higher number of used-up minutes). Give yourself 1 extra minute to get to the surface.

Assuming you can swim toward the surface at the rate of 10 feet per minute, how much time can you spend looking through the ship's wreckage before you have to start heading up?

EUCLID'S ADVICE

Write down everything you know:

- **You're 120 feet below the surface.**
- **You started out with 1 hour's worth of air in your tank, but it took you 5 minutes to get down to the wreck. That leaves you with 55 minutes of air.**
- **The first 2-minute decompression stop should be taken at half your maximum depth.**
- **You should ascend at a rate of 10 feet per minute.**
- **You have to wait 1 minute between climbs.**
- **Once you've reached a depth of 15 feet, you must stop for 5 minutes; then you can go up without any more stops.**
- **Add 1 extra minute to your time, just to be safe!**

HINT: You can use a linear equation to solve the last step in this problem.

WORKSHEET

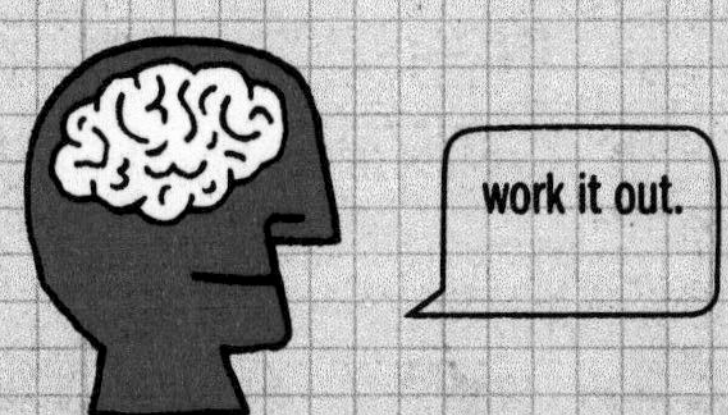
work it out.

THE SOLUTION

YOU HAVE 31 MINUTES TO EXPLORE THE WRECK BEFORE YOU HAVE TO BEGIN HEADING BACK UP TO THE SURFACE.

Solve it, step-by-step:

1. First, figure out how long it will take you to get back to the surface. It only took you 5 minutes to go down, but you didn't have to make decompression stops. Going up is a different matter. You have to add up all your decompression stops and the rate at which you're ascending. You take your first decompression stop at $\frac{1}{2}$ your maximum depth. Divide the maximum depth (120 feet) by 2 to figure out at what depth you should begin decompression stops:

$$120 \div 2 = 60 \text{ feet}$$

That means you have to take your first decompression stop at 60 feet.

2. You swim at a rate of 10 feet per minute: That's the maximum rate of ascent time that is recommended. Luckily you have your watch with you, so you can easily time your ascent to the surface. Figure out how long it will take you at this rate to get to the first decompression stop at 60 feet by dividing the number of feet you are swimming (60 feet) by the number of feet you can swim in 1 minute (10 feet).

$$60 \div 10 = 6 \text{ minutes}$$

That means it will take you 6 minutes to swim to the 60-foot marker.

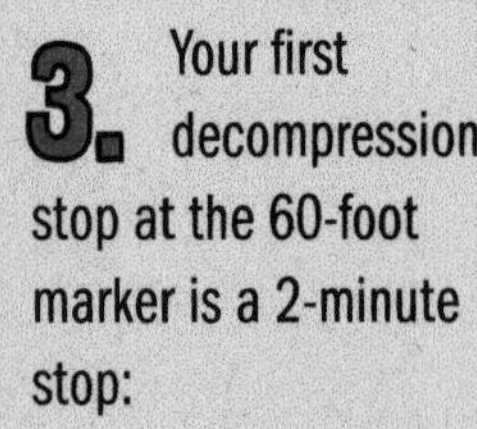

3. Your first decompression stop at the 60-foot marker is a 2-minute stop:

2 minutes

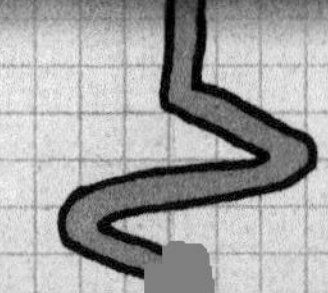

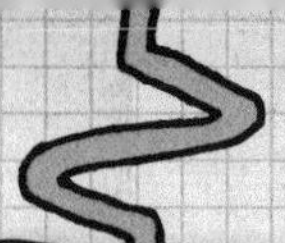

4. You then continue to ascend at a rate of 10 feet per minute until you hit the 15-foot mark, where you must make your final (and longest) decompression stop.

First, figure out how many 10-foot intervals there are between the 60-foot mark and the 15-foot mark. Subtract 15 from 60 to find out how many feet you need to swim:

$$60 - 15 = 45 \text{ feet}$$

Then, divide the difference by 10 to find out the number of intervals:

$$45 \div 10 = 4\frac{1}{2}$$

That means there are $4\frac{1}{2}$ ten-foot intervals between the 60-foot mark and the 15-foot mark. You know it takes you 1 minute to swim 10 feet, so it will take you $4\frac{1}{2}$ minutes to swim to the 15-foot mark.

$$4\frac{1}{2} \text{ minutes}$$

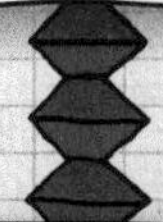

5. Here's where it gets tricky. Remember that between each 10-foot interval, you must stop for a 1-minute decompression break. But, at the 15-foot mark, you must stop for a 5-minute decompression break. That means you must add 1 extra minute for the first 4 decompression breaks, and 5 minutes for the final decompression break:

$$(4 \times 1) + 5 = 9$$

Confused? Here's how to calculate the decompression breaks:

50 feet: add a 1-minute decompression break
40 feet: add a 1-minute decompression break
30 feet: add a 1-minute decompression break
20 feet: add a 1-minute decompression break
15 feet: add a 5-minute decompression break
Total: 9 minutes

6. Now add up all the minutes it will take you, including swimming and breaks, to get to the 15-foot mark:

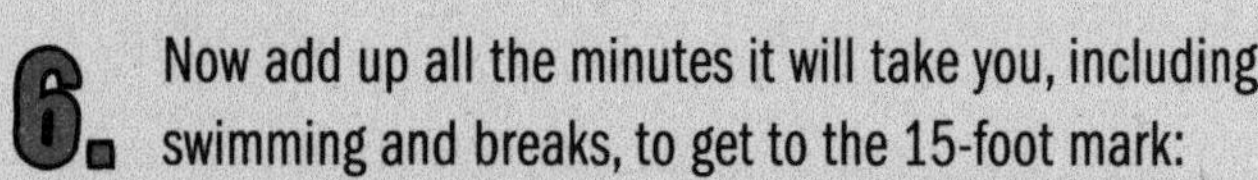

$$6 + 2 + 4\frac{1}{2} + 9 = 21\frac{1}{2} \text{ minutes}$$

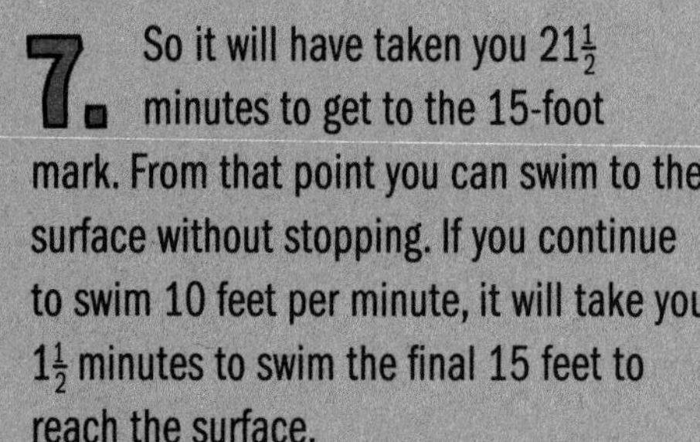

7. So it will have taken you $21\frac{1}{2}$ minutes to get to the 15-foot mark. From that point you can swim to the surface without stopping. If you continue to swim 10 feet per minute, it will take you $1\frac{1}{2}$ minutes to swim the final 15 feet to reach the surface.

$$\frac{10 \text{ feet}}{1 \text{ minute}} = \frac{15 \text{ feet}}{x \text{ minutes}}$$

$$10x = 15$$

$$x = 1\frac{1}{2} \text{ minutes}$$

8. Add up all the minutes it will take to get to the surface:

$$21\frac{1}{2} + 1\frac{1}{2} = 23 \text{ minutes}$$

Now that you know it will take you 23 minutes to get back to the surface, you can figure out how much time you have to spend searching through Redbeard's wreckage.

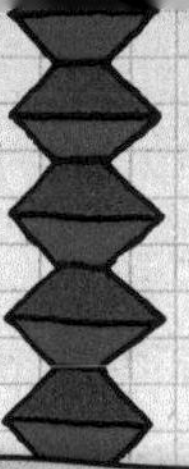

9. Set up a linear equation to solve for the amount of time you have to look for treasure. You have all of the information you need to plug in values and solve the following equation:

minutes used descending + minutes used ascending + minutes used treasure hunting = 60 (minutes spent searching for treasure)

First, assign a variable to represent the value you don't know. Let's call it *t* for treasure:

minutes used descending + minutes used ascending + t = 60 (minutes spent searching for treasure)

Next, plug in the values you do know and solve for *t*:

$$5 + 23 + t = 60$$

$$28 + t = 60$$

$$t = 32 \text{ minutes}$$

That means you have 32 minutes left to explore the wreck before you have to head up.

But wait, that's not completely right! You really only have 31 minutes of exploring. Why? Go back through the challenge.

Scuba divers are cautious, remember???

You can get an idea of how water pressure increases with depth by doing this quick and simple activity. Even in the space of 6 inches or so (the submerged portion of a drinking straw), the pressure increases. Imagine what that pressure must be like at 120 feet, or at 5 miles!

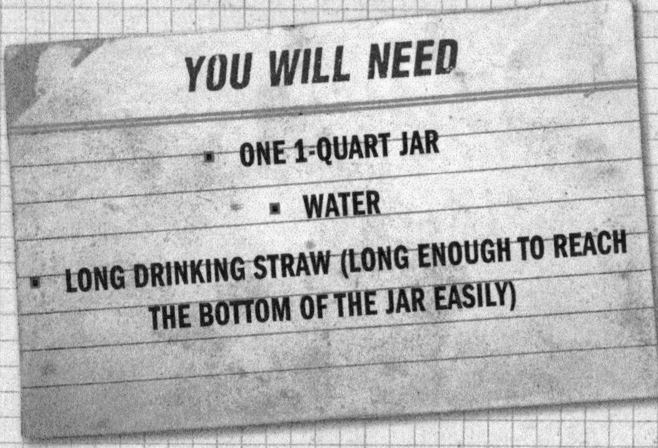

THE METHOD

1. Fill the jar almost to the top with water.

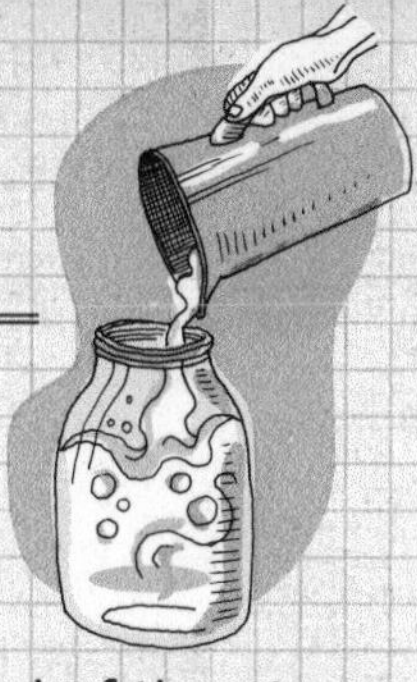

2. Put the lower end of the straw just below the surface of the water and blow. How hard or easy is it to blow bubbles?

3. Now lower the straw so that the end is at the bottom of the jar.

4. Blow again. Notice how hard or easy it is to blow bubbles.

5. Did you notice it's more difficult to blow bubbles with the straw at the bottom of the jar?

6. What can you conclude about the difference in water pressure? What does blowing bubbles at various "depths" in the container tell us about water pressure in general?

THE SOLUTION: YOU SHOULD FIND THAT THE WATER PRESSURE AT THE BOTTOM OF THE JAR IS GREATER THAN THE WATER PRESSURE AT THE TOP.

22

CHANCES OF SURVIVAL: YOU'RE DEAD

SURVIVAL STRATEGIES: RATIOS AND PROPORTIONS

DEATH BY: ENEMY SPIES

THE CHALLENGE

There's no turning back now. You and two other CIA agents have parachuted onto a snowfield high in the Himalayas. Below you it's pitch-dark, with only a few dots of a light thousands of feet below on the valley floor. Above you is the shadowy shape of the enemy spy's secret hideout. No lights come from it.

RAPPELLING

Mountain climbers often use ropes to help them on their descent using a technique called rappelling. On the way up, they will anchor one end of a rope to a rocky outcrop or other secure target. Then they do the same higher up, so the rope links to two knotted ends. When rappelling down, climbers hook a harness around their body and around the tight rope, so that the harness can slide along the tight length of rope. They slide that tight rope under one thigh, across the body, and then over the opposite shoulder. Then they jump out, letting the rope slide along their body as they briefly fall, before tightening their grip on the rope and swinging back in to the mountain.

Your team had only just worked out where this mountaintop headquarters was when you learned that Diego, one of your most respected agents, had been kidnapped by the bad guys. Your mission is to land secretly below the mountain prison, use your climbing skills to reach it, establish which room Diego is being held in, release him quickly, and get him down to the snowfield below. Then on a signal from your walkie-talkie, a helicopter will swoop around the mountain, land, and take you all to safety.

Researchers told you that the walls and doors of the headquarters are $75\frac{3}{4}$ centimeters (cm) thick. You have a special microexplosive that you can slide into the narrow slit below the door to Diego's cell. It must be slid $\frac{2}{3}$ of the way under—exactly $50\frac{1}{4}$ cm—if it's going to work. Too far and you'll injure Diego without blowing the door off. Not enough and the door won't budge, but the guards will be alerted and you'll have to leave without Diego.

After successfully breaking into the enemy spy's secret hideout, you kneel down carefully, take out the stick of explosive (no bigger than a stick of gum), and prepare to slide it under the door using the telescoping antenna of the walkie-talkie. Now all you need is the metric measuring tape to let you know when you have slid the explosive $50\frac{1}{4}$ cm of the way in. Where is it? You look frantically in your backpack while the others keep guard. It's not there!

What is there that you can use? Wait! The back of your safety belt has a measurement on it. You shine your pocket light on it, but it's not quite what you hoped for. It reads "67 cm." That's not going to help you. Or will it? The belt seems like it folds easily. You have to be exact, and you have to be quick.

What fraction of 67 cm is $50\frac{1}{4}$ cm? Can you figure out a way to use the safety belt, through a series of folds, that will allow you to find exactly $50\frac{1}{4}$ cm?

EUCLID'S ADVICE

If you could find a mark that represents exactly $50\frac{1}{4}$ cm on the belt, you could extend the antenna that far and slide the explosive under the door accurately. The key is recognizing that it will be much easier to solve this problem if you convert the numbers you do have into fractions.

Write down everything you know:

- **The 2 distances you know are the length of the belt (67 cm) and the distance you need to slide the explosive ($50\frac{1}{4}$ cm).**

WORKSHEET

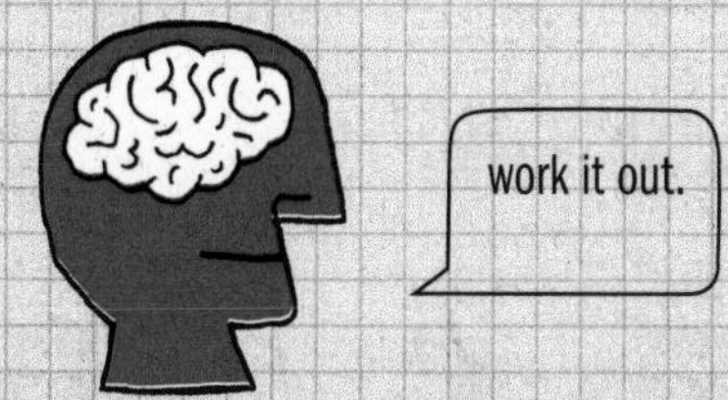
work it out.

THE SOLUTION

$50\frac{1}{4}$ CM IS $\frac{3}{4}$ OF 67 CM. YOU CAN FOLD THE BELT UNTIL IT HAS A LENGTH OF $50\frac{1}{4}$ CM.

Solve it, step-by-step:

1. The key to the solution is to use fractions, not decimals, so that you can express them in terms with a common denominator. This will allow you to easily figure out how much of the belt you should fold over to measure $50\frac{1}{4}$ cm. The simplest way to start this problem is to draw a diagram of your safety belt.

0 67 cm

Now you need to figure out where the $50\frac{1}{4}$ cm mark will be.

2. Start by figuring out the exact midway point on the belt by dividing 67 cm by 2.

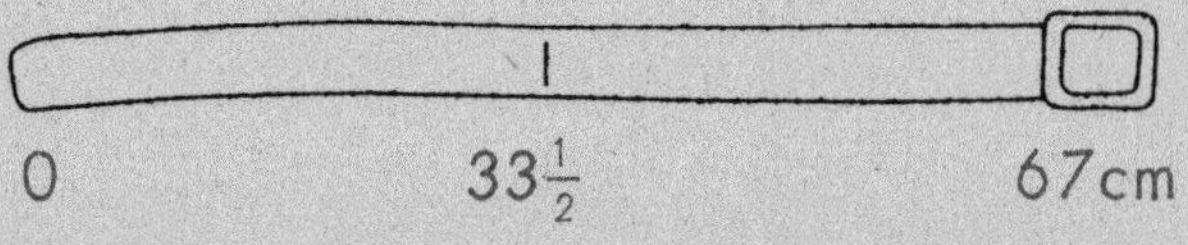

0 $33\frac{1}{2}$ 67cm

Add a mark representing $33\frac{1}{2}$ cm to your diagram.

3. Now you need to figure out where $50\frac{1}{4}$ cm is on this diagram. Based on the diagram, you can see that it looks like $50\frac{1}{4}$ cm is about halfway between the middle point and the 67-cm mark (or about $\frac{3}{4}$ of the way along this line). So let's figure out what this halfway point will look like and add 2 more notches to the diagram (before and after the midway point) by dividing the midway point ($33\frac{1}{2}$ cm) by 2.

$$33\frac{1}{2} \div 2 =$$

(rename $33\frac{1}{2}$ as $\frac{67}{2}$)	$\frac{67}{2} \div 2 =$
	$\frac{67}{2} \div \frac{2}{1} =$
(think of a division as its related multiplication problem)	$\frac{67}{2} \times \frac{1}{2} =$
(multiply the numerators and the denominators)	$\frac{67}{4}$
(rename the fraction in simplest form)	$16\frac{3}{4}$

4. That means you can add 2 new points to your diagram: $16\frac{3}{4}$ cm before the midway point, and $16\frac{3}{4}$ cm after the midway point. Add $16\frac{3}{4}$ to $33\frac{1}{2}$ to get the second number.

$$33\frac{1}{2} + 16\frac{3}{4} = 33\frac{2}{4} + 16\frac{3}{4} = 49\frac{5}{4} = 50\frac{1}{4}$$

0 $16\frac{3}{4}$ $33\frac{1}{2}$ $50\frac{1}{4}$ 67cm

5. Hey! You found the $50\frac{1}{4}$ cm notch! It's located exactly $\frac{3}{4}$ of the way along your safety belt. Alternatively, you could have set up an equation to get this answer. If *b* is the fraction of 67 cm that equals $50\frac{1}{4}$ cm, then:

$$67 \times b = 50\frac{1}{4}$$

$$b = \frac{3}{4}$$

6. Now can you figure out how to fold the belt into quarters so you can slide the explosive under the door the exact length it needs to go? Pretend a piece of scrap paper is the belt and give it a try!

- First, straighten the belt out to its full length (1).
- Next, take the right side of the belt, and fold it in half. You now have 2 equal lengths on top of each other ($\frac{1}{2} + \frac{1}{2} = 1$).
- Now grab the top length from the left side, and fold that piece in half. You've just folded one of the $\frac{1}{2}$ pieces from the previous step in half to create 2 equal $\frac{1}{4}$ pieces ($\frac{1}{2} + \frac{1}{4} + \frac{1}{4} = 1$).
- Take the last section you folded from the left side and flip that over to the right. You now have a $\frac{1}{2}$ piece of belt *plus* a $\frac{1}{4}$ piece, which adds up to $\frac{3}{4}$, which is the distance across the belt that equals $50\frac{1}{4}$ cm!

You were able to work out the calculation in the challenge pretty easily because the metric system is based on 100ths (like cents in a dollar, or percentages). And it turns out you can prepare similar challenges using our own system of lengths, which is full of twelfths, and thirty-sixths, and so on.

This lab translates the challenge into American measurements, so you can see how useful the solution is. Follow the steps to do this more familiar version, and then try working out different challenges for yourself and your friends by cutting and folding different lengths of string. (Try to cut lengths that translate into fractions—parts of 1 foot or 1 yard.)

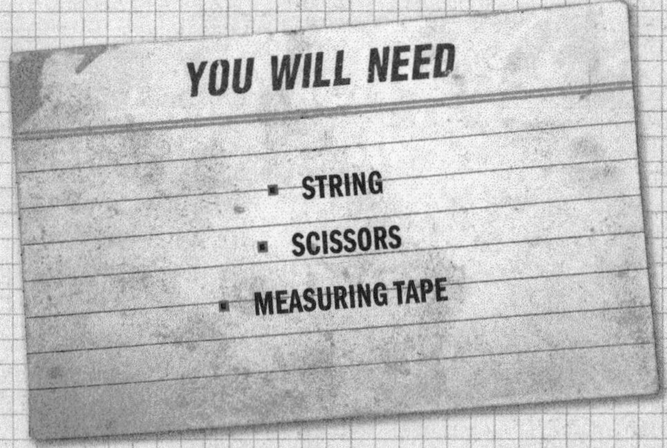

THE METHOD

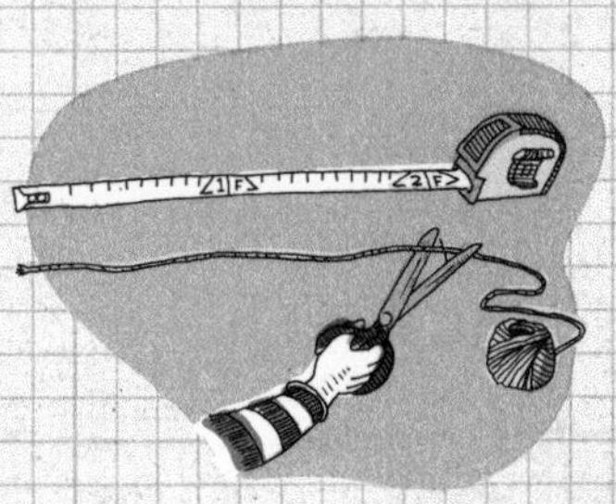

1. Measure and cut a 2-foot length of string.

2. Now give yourself the challenge of turning that into an 18-inch length of string.

HINT: 2 feet is 24 inches and 18 is $\frac{3}{4}$ of 24, so you want to find the $\frac{3}{4}$ point in the string.

3. So you're trying to turn $\frac{2}{3}$ yard into $\frac{1}{2}$ yard.

4. Repeat the challenge solution by folding the string in half, and then folding one of those halves in half . . . and then extending that second fold so that you have $\frac{3}{6}$ or $\frac{1}{2}$ of a yard.

Once you're confident enough, you can quiz your friends or create new challenges with the same technique.

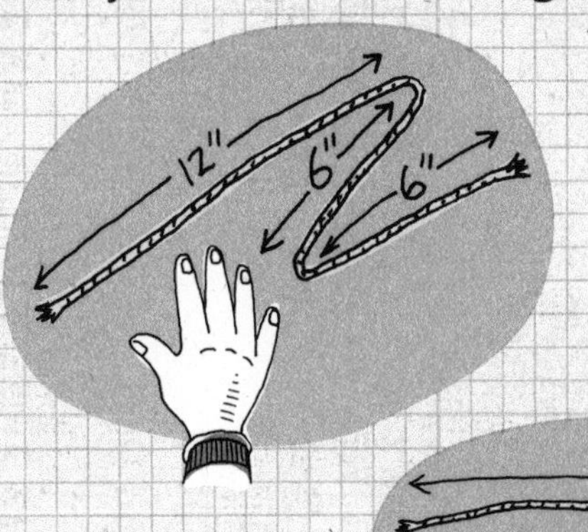

23

CHANCES OF SURVIVAL: YOU'RE DEAD

SURVIVAL STRATEGIES: EXPRESSIONS AND EQUATIONS

DEATH BY: EXECUTIONER

DEADLY TREASURE

THE CHALLENGE

You're Paolo Polo, and you've spent your life trying to match the exploits of your older brother Marco. That has meant traveling huge distances across Europe and Asia in search of adventure, wealth, and fame. You set off in 1296, just a year after Marco returned from his famous voyage, and you've been traveling for more than a decade.

MARCO POLO

Marco Polo was an Italian merchant who traveled 15,000 miles across Europe and Asia in the Middle Ages. His journey lasted 24 years and when he returned to Venice in 1295, he published *The Travels of Marco Polo*, an account of his amazing travels to Baghdad, Beijing, Constantinople, and other glittering ancient capital cities.

Which is how you wound up here, in the palace of the khan (ruler) of the Central Asian city of Samarkand. Things were going really well—guest of honor status, a lavish banquet, excellent music—until the tables were cleared. There was a feeling of expectancy and suspense in the hall.

Then you were led to the center of the hall, where you now stand. Ahead of you is a strange display. In the middle are three jewel-encrusted chests of different sizes, although even the smallest is larger than a young elephant. To the left of the chests hang three keys, one for each chest. To the right is an executioner, holding his gleaming ax, and an hourglass with sand filtering through it.

That's when things take a different—and much scarier—turn. Your host, the khan, tells you that you may have all three keys, and the contents of the chests, if you can give the exact weight of each chest before the last grain of sand passes through the hourglass. If you fail, he adds, the executioner will cut off your head. He will give you 1 minute on the hourglass.

Things seem pretty hopeless, until the khan gives you a clue. The smallest chest and the middle chest, added together, weigh 50,000 tekels. The largest and the smallest weigh 60,000 tekels, whereas the largest and the middle chest combined weigh 70,000 tekels.

Then he orders the executioner to wait until all the sand has passed from the top of the glass (which it's about to do in a few seconds), and then flip the glass over, and start timing the 1 minute. So you'd better do some calculations fast!

Can you figure out the exact weight of each chest?

EUCLID'S ADVICE

Don't let yourself get thrown by that funny word "tekel." It is simply a unit of measure, like pounds or ounces, that is used by the khan to measure weight. If you find it easier, imagine the amounts to be in pounds, kilograms, or even marbles:

- **First, try to simplify the problem. One source of confusion might be that you're dealing with big numbers—in the tens of thousands. If you find and divide each number by the highest common factor (in this case it's 10,000), the numbers become much simpler to work with. Just be sure to multiply each answer by the same factor at the end!**

- **Now things look a little different:**

– The weight of the smallest and the middle chest add up to 5.

– The weight of the smallest and the largest add up to 6.

– The weight of the middle and the largest add up to 7.

HINT: Assigning variables to represent each of the chests will help you.

WORKSHEET

work it out.

THE SOLUTION

THE SMALLEST CHEST WEIGHS 20,000 TEKELS, THE MIDDLE WEIGHS 30,000 TEKELS, AND THE LARGEST WEIGHS 40,000 TEKELS.

Solve it, step-by-step:

1. First, let's assign variables to represent each chest.

a = weight of the smallest chest

b = weight of the middle chest

c = weight of the largest chest

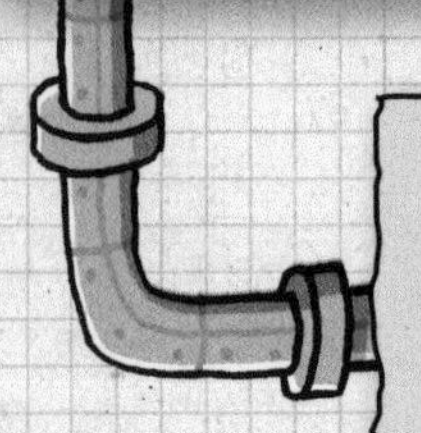

2. Next, let's write out equations to represent what we know about the weights of the chests.

$$a + b = 50{,}000$$

$$a + c = 60{,}000$$

$$b + c = 70{,}000$$

3. Since these numbers are all divisible by 10,000 (the highest common factor), let's knock off four zeros on each number to make our calculations simpler. Just remember to add them back on at the very end.

$$a + b = 5$$

$$a + c = 6$$

$$b + c = 7$$

4. Now here's where you need to think logically about the useful information you can infer from these equations. Let's look at the first two equations:

Each contains two variables.

Each contains the variable *a*, which means that the sum differs because the value of *b* and *c* are not equal.

In fact, when you replace the value *b* with *c*, the sum is one more.

That means that *c* weighs one more than *b*, so you can now represent the value of *c* as $b + 1$, or $c = b + 1$.

5. Now you can rewrite the third equation this way:

$$b + b + 1 = 7$$

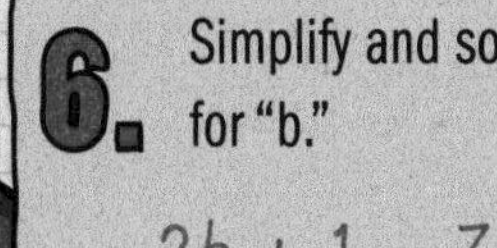

6. Simplify and solve for "b."

$$2b + 1 = 7$$
$$2b = 6$$
$$b = 3$$

7. Since you know the value of "b," you can also solve for "c" and "a."

$$c = b + 1$$
$$c = 3 + 1$$
$$c = 4$$

$$a + b = 5$$
$$a + 3 = 5$$
$$a = 2$$

8. But, wait! You're not quite done yet. Don't forget to multiply each weight by the highest common factor (10,000).

a = 20,000 tekels

b = 30,000 tekels

c = 40,000 tekels

That wasn't so bad! Did you beat the clock and escape with the treasure?

MATH LAB

One of the secrets to solving this challenge is being able to make large numbers more manageable—by dividing and multiplying by the highest common factor. You can do that in all sorts of situations. In fact, you can even re-create the whole solar system in your nearest park!

Try this activity to get a real idea of how far each planet is from the Sun. You might be surprised to learn just how far the Sun is from some of our neighbors. It's more fun if you can get hold of different balls and pieces of fruit to act as planet models (they give you an idea of the relative sizes of the planets). But if you can't rustle up all of them, you can still enjoy this experiment using whatever markers you can find.

Just make sure that you have enough space, because one of your measurements will be almost 300 feet long.

YOU WILL NEED

- STICK OR CANE (TO BE USED AS A MARKER)
- TAPE MEASURE
- GOLF BALL
- PENCIL
- PAPER
- TENNIS BALL
- BASEBALL
- TANGERINE
- BEACH BALL
- BASKETBALL
- GRAPEFRUIT
- SOFTBALL

THE METHOD

1. Find a spot in a park where you will have a long expanse of level ground (up to 300 feet).

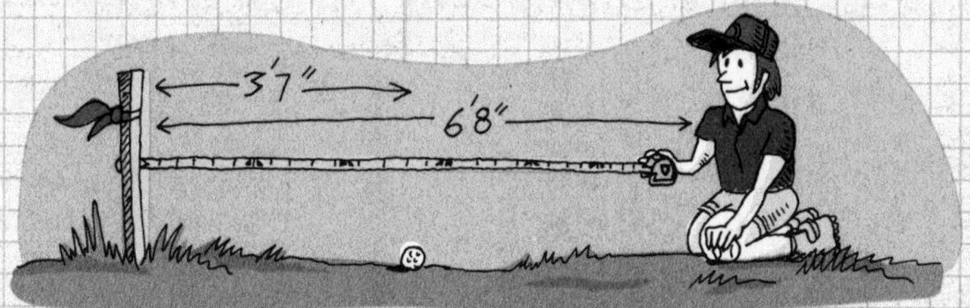

2. Put the stick or other marker into the ground: This will be the Sun in your solar system model.

3. Begin measuring from the Sun until you reach 3 feet, 7 inches, which equals approximately 3.6 feet (remember, there are 12 inches in 1 foot; $\frac{7}{12}$ = approximately 0.6); put a golf ball here to act as Mercury. Mark this distance (3.6 feet) down on your paper, and do the same each time you place a new planet.

4. Go back to the Sun. Continue measuring and put a tennis ball down at 6 feet, 8 inches (6.7 feet) from the Sun to act as Venus.

5. The baseball represents Earth at 9 feet, 4 inches (9.3 feet) from the Sun.

6. At 14 feet from the Sun, mark Mars with the tangerine.

7. At 48 feet from the Sun, mark Jupiter with the beach ball.

8. At 89 feet from the Sun, mark Saturn with the basketball.

9. At 178 feet from the Sun, mark Uranus with the grapefruit.

10. At 280 feet from the Sun, mark Neptune with the softball.

11. You now have all eight planets lined up in their relative distance from the Sun. Now look at your list of planets and multiply all of your distances by 10,000,000 and change the units from feet to miles (this is the same as moving the decimal place 7 times). Those new numbers indicate the number of miles (not feet) each planet is from the Sun.

Sample page from your notes:

Planet	**Distance from the Sun (in lab experiment)**	**Actual distance from the Sun**
Mercury	3.6 feet	36,000,000 miles
Venus	6.7 feet	67,000,000 miles

Amazing, isn't it?!

BRAIN BENDER

CAN 2 = 1?

Here's an Einstein-level challenge. Start with this statement:

$$a = b$$

Using that starting point, here are a series of equations that will lead to the unlikely conclusion that 2 = 1.

$$a = b$$
$$a^2 = ab$$
$$a^2 - b^2 = ab - b^2$$
$$(a + b)(a - b) = b(a - b)$$
$$a + b = b$$
$$2b = b$$
$$2 = 1$$

Now, can you find the flaw in the logic that led to the conclusion that 2 = 1? In other words, explain where this apparently logical argument makes a step which is not valid. (Hint: What can you say about $a - b$?)

The Solution: Remember the hint? Well, if $a = b$, then $a - b$ is zero. Now the first 4 equations led up neatly to the introduction of that term. And the next equation calls for dividing each side by $(a - b)$, but dividing by zero isn't possible—and so are the chances of getting 2 to equal 1.

1
2
3

24

CHANCES OF SURVIVAL: YOU'RE DEAD

SURVIVAL STRATEGIES: PROBABILITY

DEATH BY: BEHEADING

WHICH DOOR TO CHOOSE?

THE CHALLENGE

It was no use trying to persuade the duke's guards that you were entirely innocent, and that it was another young person in a crimson cloak who had beheaded the statue of the duke outside the castle walls. The duke became furious when he learned of the act, and the guards knew that their own lives would be in danger if they didn't return with the culprit.

THE MONTY HALL PROBLEM

Monty Hall was the co-creator of the popular TV game show *Let's Make a Deal* and hosted the show on and off for nearly 20 years. One of the biggest attractions of the show was watching contestants decide what's hidden behind the three doors on the stage. Will it be a fantastic prize like a trip to Europe or will it be a worthless booby prize, called a "zonk"?

Contestants were always offered the chance to switch their choice of door—just like in our challenge. The public became so fascinated with the "switch or stay" question that it became known—even to college math professors—as the Monty Hall Problem.

So now you find yourself being marched into the banquet hall. The dozens of people at the tables stop their eating and talking as you are led straight to the table below the tapestry.

There the duke sits, staring at you, furious. "I, Don Carlo, rule as far as the eye can see," he says. "I rule justly, and my people respect and obey me because I bring them peace and plenty. We are like a family, which is why an act committed against me is an act against us all. And it must be punished accordingly."

He continues, "I could have you executed straight away but I desire entertainment—and can also offer you a chance to save your life. Look beyond me and you will see three doors—numbered 1, 2, and 3. One of them leads to your freedom. The other two lead to the executioner's porch. You must choose a door."

Terrified, you eventually summon up the energy to utter the words, "Door number 2."

The duke, with a playful yet cruel expression on his face, says, "Open door number 1."

The door opens, and you see a staircase leading down into the darkness. Obviously it is one of the two executioner's doors. The duke chuckles darkly and says, "You would have lost your life if you had chosen that door. You must choose once more. I will let you switch your choice to door number 3 if you so desire. Will you switch or will you stay with door number 2?"

The decision is yours. If you switch doors, what are the odds you'll choose the door to freedon?

PROBABILITY

Probability is the chance that something will or will not happen. Let's take a coin toss as an example. A coin has two sides: heads and tails. When you flip a coin, it can only land on one of those two sides. So, the odds of landing on tails are 1 out of 2 (or $\frac{1}{2}$, or 50 percent). Keep in mind that probability describes what is likely to happen over many, many flips of a coin. It isn't a guarantee that if you flip twice, you will always get one head and one tail. But if you flip it 500 times, for example, you should expect about 250 to be heads and about 250 to be tails.

EUCLID'S ADVICE

This challenge hinges on probability. You need to examine the odds (probability) at each stage.

Write down everything you know:

- **To begin with, you had a 1 out of 3 chance of choosing a door to freedom.**
- **When the duke opened door number 1 and gave you the chance to switch, he reduced the number of doors to 2.**

Still confused? Try doing the Math Lab on page 232 first—it will help you understand the probability involved in this challenge.

HINT: Draw a table or a tree diagram to map out your choices.

WORKSHEET

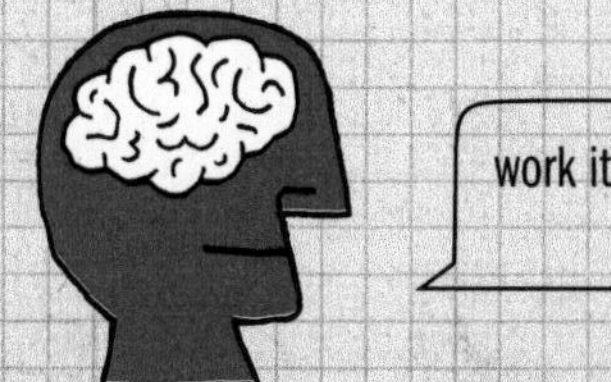
work it out.

THE SOLUTION

THE ODDS OF CHOOSING THE DOOR TO FREEDOM ARE $\frac{2}{3}$ IF YOU SWITCH DOORS. THAT MEANS YOU DOUBLE YOUR CHANCES OF SAVING YOURSELF BY SWITCHING DOORS.

Solve it, step-by-step:

1. At first, the probability that each door will lead to freedom is the same: a one out of three ($\frac{1}{3}$) chance. In other words, your choice (door number 2) had a one out of three ($\frac{1}{3}$) chance and doors 1 and 3 *between them* had a two out of three ($\frac{2}{3}$) chance.

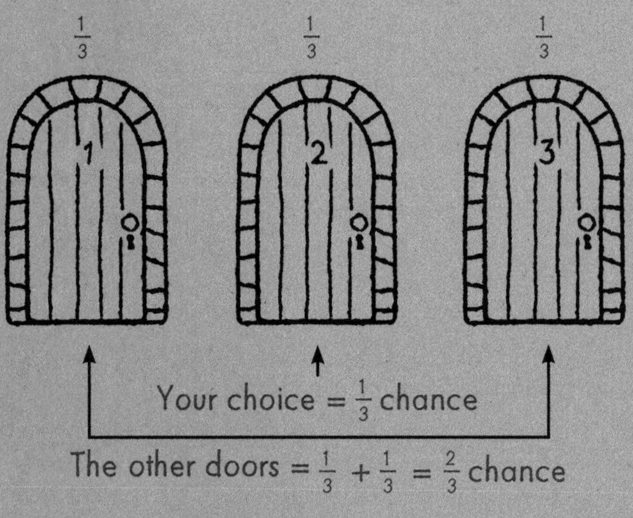

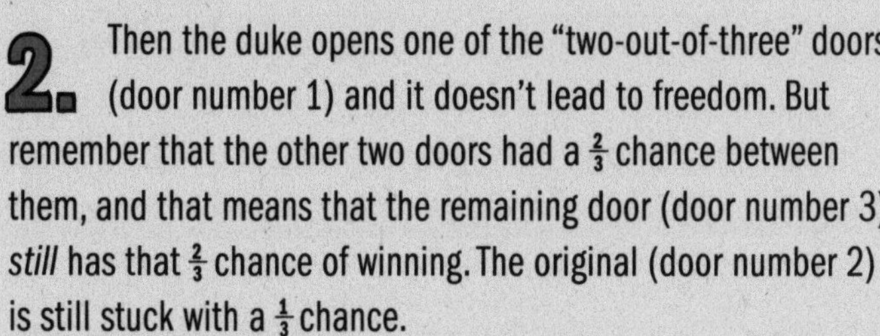

2. Then the duke opens one of the "two-out-of-three" doors (door number 1) and it doesn't lead to freedom. But remember that the other two doors had a $\frac{2}{3}$ chance between them, and that means that the remaining door (door number 3) *still* has that $\frac{2}{3}$ chance of winning. The original (door number 2) is still stuck with a $\frac{1}{3}$ chance.

3. That means that switching doors doubles your chances of succeeding!

Want to prove that this really works? Do the Math Lab on the next page and you can show everyone that switching doors really does double your chances of survival!

MATH LAB

Part of the fun for viewers of the old television game show called *Let's Make a Deal* was trying to work out the odds of winning big—or losing. Monty Hall, the host, would often open one of the three doors to the contestant and offer the player the chance to switch their choice of door. The contestant got to keep whatever prize was behind the door of their choosing.

You can do your own version of Monty's approach with some prizes—and gag prizes, or zonks—of your own. Get some friends to play along and keep track of how often players win and lose if they switch their choice. The results might surprise you—and anyone else who doesn't believe the answer to the challenge. (And that group even contains a few math professors!)

YOU WILL NEED

- SEVERAL FRIENDS TO PLAY THE GAME
- 3 LARGE PAPER OR PLASTIC CUPS
- TABLE OR COUNTER TO PUT THE CUPS ON
- 10 TO 20 SMALL CANDY BARS (OR OTHER SMALL "PRIZES")
- 2 SMALL PLASTIC FIGURES, SMALL ENOUGH TO FIT UNDER THE CUPS (THE UGLIER THE BETTER—THESE ARE THE ZONKS IN YOUR GAME)
- PENCIL
- PAPER

THE METHOD

You will need to play the role of Monty Hall, the host of this game show.

1. With none of your friends looking, set the cups upside down on the table.

2. Put a candy bar or other small prize under one of the cups and a zonk under each of the other two. *Important*: You must remember which is which!

3. Ask a friend to choose one of the cups for the prize.

4. Now turn over one of the other two cups (making sure you choose a zonk) and ask whether your friend wants to switch their choice of cup.

5. Turn over the cup they choose (either switching or not) and record whether they won or not—and whether they switched.

6. Repeat steps 3 through 5 with another friend.

7. Play the game 10 or 12 times.

8. Compare how many times players won if they switched, with how many times they won by sticking with their first choices. You'll see just how the solution for "Which Door to Choose?" makes sense!

INDEX

100
90
80
70
60
50
40
30
20
10

WORKSHEET

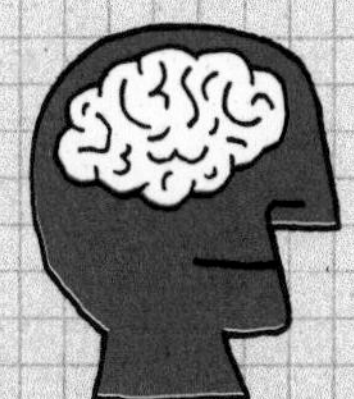

work it out.

WORKSHEET

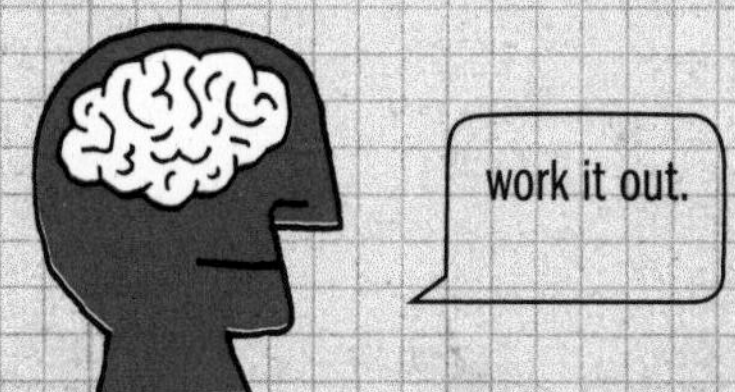
work it out.

WORKSHEET

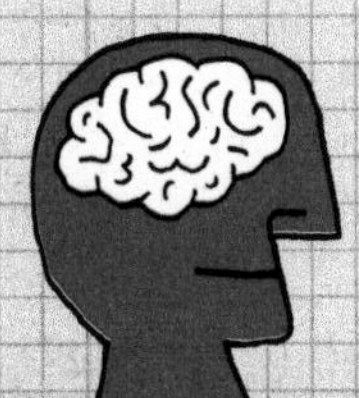
work it out.

WORKSHEET